A *history of*
MARKEATON
and
MACKWORTH

From Mearca to Clark-Maxwell

A *history of*
MARKEATON
and
MACKWORTH

by Don Farnsworth

breedon **books**
PUBLISHING

First published in Great Britain in 2006 by
The Breedon Books Publishing Company Limited
Breedon House, 3 The Parker Centre,
Derby, DE21 4SZ.

ISBN 1 85983 503 1

Printed and bound by Biddles Ltd, King's Lynn, Norfolk.

Contents

Dedication

This book is dedicated to the men who, in the year 1086 on the orders of King William I, made the assessment of this manor and, in a few terse phrases, all unknowingly gave us the first recorded glimpse of our historical heritage – the Domesday Book.

This edition is also gratefully dedicated to the treasured memories of Tom Bond, who was organist at All Saints Church, Mackworth for 76 years and of Nora Harland, chorister and friend to many.

Acknowledgements

I WISH to place on record my thanks to the numerous people and organisations without whom this publication would not have been possible. As this edition uses much of the text and all of the illustrations from the first one, this list must necessarily include those people who generously contributed in any way to the earlier version plus a number of others whose later contributions are also gratefully received. It is a source of considerable regret that some of these names are now prefixed with the word 'late', but a lot of years have passed since the first edition.

My sincere thanks then to all the following: to the late Revd H.A. Dane, who first inspired the idea, for permission to use the map and extracts from the church guide and for help with local knowledge; also for much supportive encouragement. To Maxwell Craven, who contributed much to the family pedigrees and for directing me to many sources of valuable information. To the late Dr G.S. Clark-Maxwell for allowing me to take photographs on his property and for local and family information; also for his later personal addition to my store of local knowledge which appears at the end of this book. To his daughter, Dr Priscilla Hamilton, for her valuable help sorting out the family tree and for hospitality. To Charles Clark-Maxwell for much family and local information, for allowing me to photograph portraits of his ancestors and for access to the 1930 sale catalogue for Markeaton Hall and other books. Also for his enthusiasm during long sessions of photography in the church, during which he showed me important details there to which I had perhaps been too close, too often, to have observed properly. To the former county archivist Miss Joan Sinar and her successor Dr Margaret O'Sullivan and the staff at the County Record Office who gave considerable help with the map and other documentary information. Since the first edition Rosemary Lucas has written three complementary publications on details such as population, enclosures etc, and her meticulous research has been invaluable for this edition. (see *Bibliography*). Special thanks to Andrew Polkey for the opportunity to study and copy the Markeaton Document (see *Introduction*) and to Joan D'Arcy for her invaluable help and expertise with the transcription.

I remain indebted to Miss Sylvia Bown, Lisa Bates and Michael Thornton, all formerly of Derby Local Studies Library, and more recently Trish Kenny, Paul Hudson and their colleagues, for access to much valuable material and for facilities for photography without which the inclusion of some of the following illustrations would not have been possible; also to David Fraser, former Chief Museums Officer for Derby and his successor Anneke Bamberry, Jonathan Platt, formerly Keeper of Derby Industrial Museum and Mr Peter Gratton, former County Librarian, for permission to publish pictures in their care. I also thank Mr R.E. Lassam, formerly Curator of the Fox Talbot Museum at Lacock, Wiltshire, for his specialist knowledge and help. To Les Whittaker my thanks for the generous gift of the text books by Frederick Haynes (see *Varieties* with regard to education).

To those people, many of them local, who so enthusiastically contributed information and/or photographs or helped in practical ways, I owe much. They include the late Miss Arnett and Mrs Pride, Revd Canon Michael Austin, Mrs Blythe, the late Peter Brady, Maureen Bull, Barbara Bryer, the late Mary Campbell, Molly and Philip Clark, Revd John Drackley, Ann and Stephen Derbyshire, Dr A.E. and Mrs E.M. Dodd, Adrian Farnsworth, June and Ken Foster, Mrs J. Fuller, John Hammersley, Mrs Anne Haslam, Margaret James and the late Donald James, Mrs A. Kirkland, Mary and Peter Knight, Mrs L.F. Litherland, Rosemary and the late John Lucas, Ron McKeown, Revd Dr Ian Mitchell, Alan Oldfield, Beryl Olpin, Parochial Church Council of All Saints Mackworth, the late Eileen Sharp, Vivienne Smith, Pamela Storer and Richard Wood.

I am grateful to the undermentioned establishments for the use of text or illustrations in their possession: Derbyshire Archaeological Society for the extract from the Derbyshire Archaeological Journal Vol. 51, 1930; Cambridge University Collection of Air Photographs; Derbyshire County Council for use of the vertical aerial photographs; H. Tempest (Cardiff) Ltd for free use of the aerial photograph of Markeaton Hall; W.W. Winter, Derby Museum and Art Gallery and Derby City Leisure Services Department. These last two were especially generous and helpful in their assistance with illustrations, as were the *Derby Evening Telegraph,* whose extensive archives produced most of the photographs of Markeaton Hall as well as others of historic interest. Derby is indeed fortunate to have a newspaper which puts so much emphasis on local history and even prints a regular special edition, the 'Bygones'. On a practical note I thank my late former working colleague Bryan Warren for producing the original family tree artwork (which I have now updated) and Mrs Janet Stills who, for the first edition, converted my multicoloured hieroglyphics into orderly typescript; having since learned to type to a modest degree myself I now fully appreciate what she achieved. Finally, but certainly not least, my gratitude to my wife Barbara for her unceasing patience and support in this project.

Don Farnsworth
March 2006

Introduction

THE BASIC history of our country, both physical and political, is fairly well known and much literature has been published on the subject. Most of our cities and towns have also had their individual histories published but, in between, there are the villages and hamlets, many of which are a thousand or more years old, of which little is known or written about, yet it is these which form the background against which all the rest is set.

Awareness of this fact is definitely on the increase, especially over the last 30 years or so, and more people are turning to writing this type of village history which, individually, may be of only local interest but collectively must help to build up the overall picture, and it is to this end that the first edition of this book was produced in 1987. Now, with more information and many more illustrations (and some corrections!) available it seems worthwhile publishing a new version. It is still not intended as an exhaustive history but hopefully it will give a better idea of the development of these two communities and their legacy to us. We are, after all, only the temporary custodians of what is around us and a knowledge of our past may help us to appreciate our inheritance and to preserve it in turn for future generations. We have already lost far too much.

Detail for this sort of history is difficult to come by. One reason is that most of it was trivial by national standards during a long period when only the most important events and people merited any form of record and even then we have to accept that some of the little we do know may not be accurate.

As an example, as late as the 16th century the relatively simple matter of John Mundy acquiring the Manor of Markeaton has three versions, only one of which seems to have been contemporaneously documented. Unfortunately it is part of this very version, concerning the advowson or patronage of the church, which clashes with other previously believed history and we are left wondering how reliable the documentation was and which version (if any) is the correct one.

The previous paragraph was written for the first edition and basically is still relevant. However, in April 2005 the author was shown a document which had recently been found. It is in the form of a small book (about A5 size) of 12 pages of very thin, fragile paper, the last three of which are blank, glued into a parchment cover. It is badly damaged around the edges and large pieces of the first page are missing. At the request of the finder it has now been passed to Derby Local Studies Library where it is listed as MSS BV 900. In the absence of any official title it will be referred to hereafter as the Markeaton Document.

It seems to be a draft or copy of something larger as there are references in the margins to items which do not appear in these pages. It is mainly damaged on the right-hand side and some text is missing. The left-hand pages have wide margins so that, with the exception of the first left-hand leaf, which has about one third missing, the script is largely undamaged. The first (left-hand) leaf is a genealogical table of the first four generations of the Mundy family to own Markeaton. The top and much of the left side of this page is missing, but it is clearly dated to February 1599. There is no indication as to the identity of the writer.

The much damaged first page is a family tree of the Mundys from Sir John down to Edward and his children and includes some names that were previously uncertain. The rest of the document is concerned mainly with the family history and contains some interesting details which will appear later in the text under *Lords of the Manor*.

There is actually another version of the story concerning a Mr Noon from whom John Mundy reputedly purchased the estate and as a result was thereafter known as Mundy after Noon! In the first edition the credibility of such a situation was put in doubt, but in common with many unlikely tales the truth has emerged and been proved to be based on fact. The true version occurred 300 years after John Mundy acquired Markeaton and also in another county; in fact in Leicestershire at Burton Hall near Loughborough, which was owned by a Mr Noon. He was very friendly with the Mundys and, being childless, he took a fancy to Charles Godfrey, the younger son of Francis Mundy, to such an extent that he made young Charles his heir and in due course, early in the 19th century, Charles inherited the Burton estate and really did become Mundy after Noon! Which shows how careful one must be when writing history; there is a pitfall round every corner. Because of this sort of situation and in spite of what has been learned since the first edition, it is still virtually certain that this book contains as yet unrecognised errors which derive from various sources for a variety of reasons, but their inclusion here is accepted as the sole responsibility of the author.

The lack of reliable sources has caused numerous problems in the compiling of even these few pages. All too often words to the effect of 'we do not know' occur because there really is nothing else to say in the circumstances. Equally overworked, in spite of severe editing, are the words 'possible', 'probable' and 'may', but there are times when there seems to be no alternative. For all our extensive knowledge of the past it is notable that if we were to treat each known historical fact as a building block, and if the blocks were to be assembled in chronological order to build a hypothetical wall, we should find ourselves looking at a lot more space than wall. However, it is hoped that the result will still be of sufficient interest to have been worthwhile. Another word which appears all too frequently in these pages, but for which there seems little alternative, is 'demolished'.

Except for the photographs which were taken specifically for this book there are as many old and rarely published prints and photographs as could be reasonably included. The inferior quality of some of these photographs is due to their being copied from old originals which are now in a very poor state of preservation. Also included this time are vertical aerial views of the manor.

The pedigrees of the four families who have owned the manor have, for the sake of space and clarity, been reduced to the direct line of descent (plus those people who are relevant to the text) and for no longer than they resided in the manor. That of the Clark-Maxwells has been brought up to date as they are fortunately still resident.

Although there is a short section on prehistory, the real substance of this book begins with the building of a Roman road and ends, perhaps appropriately, with a modern one.

A list of books used for reference and some others which are suitable for further reading is included.

The Map

The original of this map is held by the Derbyshire Record Office at Matlock, along with the very large parchment scroll which carries the key to the relevant features on it. Although apparently drawn in about 1740 it shows the new enclosure awards of 1760–1763 in addition to some existing enclosures which remained intact. Fortunately for us, it includes details which were gone by that date (i.e. the old Markeaton Hall, which was replaced c.1755, and the village which was cleared when the park was landscaped). It also omits the changes in the road system which should have occurred after the Turnpike Act of 1738, so we get a very good idea of the area as it was in the mid-18th century. Burdett's map of 1767 does show such changes, and considering the time he took on his survey, these must have been effected some years before this map's publication date. No special maps were prepared for the enclosures and this one of 1740 and the 1737 one of Allestree were simply adapted for the occasion.

The original shows the field numbers of the old and new enclosures, but as some of them did not reproduce satisfactorily they have been deleted here for the sake of clarity, as have numerous pencil additions which seem to have no immediate relevance. They would, in any case, have made the small scale reproduction used here seem very cluttered.

Even without these the map is of considerable interest for the physical features it shows, such as the late mediaeval road system, the villages and the water courses. Many of the fields still exist in the same form today. Perhaps its most valuable asset, apart from the wealth of detail, is its accuracy compared to the modern OS map. The scale quoted (in later pencil) is approximately 18 chains to one inch, but its actual scale is 16.8 chains to one inch or four and three-quarter inches to one mile. For the purposes of this book it has been reduced to two and a half inches to one mile so that direct comparison can be made to the OS map of that scale.

Due to the prevailing circumstances this was reproduced from a good quality photocopy and has undergone some necessary redrawing, although reference was made to the original for the sake of accuracy and authenticity. The two maps of the villages which appear later have also been enlarged and redrawn from the photocopy to show as much detail as possible.

CHAPTER ONE

Markeaton and Mackworth

Prehistory

There is very little evidence available to tell us of the situation in prehistoric times in the immediate area of Derby. A few miles away in the Trent Valley there is abundant evidence, from aerial photographs and excavation, of man's occupation from the Neolithic period (c.3000–2000BC) onward, but a little to the north the land changes from gravel to clay and hardly any trace of early man remains.

Apart from the Trent Valley the nearest known prehistoric site to Derby is (or was before it was ploughed out) a barrow, or burial mound, at Hungry Bentley 10 miles to the west. In the vicinity of Derby there have been, over many years, finds of artifacts such as flint arrow heads and stone implements among the more recent of which are a stone hammer head at Chaddesden in 1980 and a greenstone axe from Langdale, Cumbria, found in the road workings near Markeaton Park in 1983. A very well-preserved socketed bronze axe head was found at Allestree in 1978 while another stone hammer head came from the bed of the River Derwent near Little Chester.

While these items do not prove that man actually settled here, we can be fairly safe in assuming that he did, as virtually the whole of the rest of Derbyshire bears signs of his presence. These consist of habitation sites traceable from the air in the Trent gravels, remains of stone-based structures in the Peak district and evidence of cave dwellings. There are also some field systems and numerous burial sites. However, any trace of the flimsy thatched huts in this area will long ago have been erased by the continual cultivation and building over the many ensuing centuries. In Neolithic times farmers cleared areas of forest for crop cultivation and this may have occurred locally, as the ancient name of Brun Lane at Mackworth indicates burning at some point.

Certainly there were trade routes and one of these, the Portway, passed close by at Little Eaton on its way from the north of the country to the River Trent at Nottingham. There may have been a route to the west from the Derby area into Cheshire for salt, but to date this is pure speculation and is based on the idea that the Roman road, which came later, could have followed the line of an existing trackway. Apart from these few items we are left with the frustrating fact that we know very little of prehistoric activity in this area.

Roman

In AD43 the Emperor Claudius's troops landed in Kent and proceeded to subjugate the numerous tribes of natives who occupied the country. Some of these tribes already had pro-Roman rulers, some submitted fairly easily, but others fought on and it was four to five years before the Romans reached this area and built a fort on a hilltop overlooking the River Derwent in the part of Derby now covered by Belper Road and Derwent Park. Some years later in around AD80 they moved to a site on the east side of the river and built a more substantial structure which eventually had stone walls, the foundations of which still lie buried at Little Chester (Roman Derventio). Around this grew a large *vicus* or civil settlement for trade and industry.

Having established themselves the Romans linked their various positions across the country with a network of well-made roads, one of which went almost due west from Little Chester to Rocester, 15 miles away, where they had another fort. The line of this road is lost for the first three miles from Little Chester but for the sake of this book we can assume that it went straight from the fort, through the two manors where there is some evidence to show its alignment, to the point in the fields beyond Brun Lane at Mackworth from where it becomes traceable for most of its way to Rocester. From Rocester the road turned north-west to pass through the salt producing area near Northwich on its way to Chester and the coast.

This road is important in the history of Markeaton and Mackworth as both villages seem to have originally been centred on or very near to it and certainly, for much of the time since, it has been used as a connecting link between the two. Even today a much-used footpath closely follows the line through the fields. The Romans were here for about four centuries but we have no evidence that either of the villages was founded in that period, although the possibility is there. It is well known that there was integration with the natives, not infrequently resulting in marriage, and beyond doubt some soldiers, on retirement from the army, settled here and farmed the land. There are known Roman settlement sites at nearby Mickleover, with some traces at Humbleton and also at Thurvaston a few miles to the west; in such good agricultural country there must surely be others awaiting discovery. There was certainly one near Mackworth which has been found by metal detecting, but to date the exact location has not been divulged even for the sake of the historical record.

Figurines of two Roman gods found on the estate. *(Author)*

Saxon to 1066

The Romans remained in Britain until the beginning of the fifth century when they withdrew to support their crumbling empire elsewhere. From then on the invading Saxons gradually spread over the countryside. In spite of their warlike reputation they were basically rural settlers and farmers who tended to settle away from the Roman roads, although they would not have been averse to taking over the many well-established Roman farms even near the roads. They did little to maintain the high-class road system the Romans had built and much of it was allowed to deteriorate to trackways or was even simply used as a ready-made boundary which, as we shall see later, possibly happened here.

During the ensuing centuries, the so-called Dark Ages, many such settlements were established, each ruled by its head man or Lord, from whom the village often took its name. Derby itself is an amalgam of several villages, Northworthy (north enclosure), Alvaston (Alwald's farm), Boulton (Bola's farm) and Osmaston (Osmund's farm) being examples. Northworthy was the central village, being based on the confluence of the River Derwent and the Markeaton Brook. The Vikings who came in the ninth century changed the name completely and Northworthy became Deoraby (the place of deer or deer clearing) from which there is the obvious simplification over the years to Derby. Also, during this period, a system of taxation was introduced based on the ownership of land, taking into account both the quantity owned and the quality of the soil in any given area. For taxable purposes shires were divided into 'hundreds', which were groups of estates adding up to a hundred 'hides', the hide being a measurement of land equivalent to approximately 120 acres. No one was exempt and by the time the Normans arrived this system was so well established that they had little difficulty in adapting it when compiling that dreaded catalogue, the Domesday Book, and each entry carries the taxable value of pre-1086 as well as the new value.

A little over a mile to the west of Northworthy the Roman road crossed the brook and near this crossing point a Saxon 'ton' or farm settlement was founded. This was almost certainly Mearca's ton, although there are two other possible origins of the name Markeaton. They are 'village on the boundary stream', which is at least geographically feasible, and 'Marsh Farm', a version for which there is no positive evidence. However, Mearca's Farm seems to be the more probable version as only a mile to the west was Macca's Worth, or enclosure. As the earliest written record of these places is the Domesday Book of 1086, and as much of the information in it was gathered verbally, and as spellings of the same place name varied considerably even in the same book, it does seem possible, even probable, that Mearca and Macca were one and the same person. Land was a valuable asset and it seems perfectly logical that, having established an estate, the next move was to enclose more adjacent land to enlarge the estate. Whether this is true or not, one thing is certain, that Domesday is the first positive record of Markeaton and Mackworth and it is from this time that we can start to trace their history.

Norman

After the departure of the Romans the Saxons did not immediately overrun the country. The establishment of the basic pattern of settlements as we know them took hundreds of years but, nonetheless, it is probable that when William, Duke of Normandy, landed in 1066 and proclaimed himself king, some of the towns and settlements in his newly acquired territory were already over 500 years old. When William arrived the country was divided between numerous local earls and other manorial overlords of varying degrees of status and power. Very early on in his reign William stamped his authority on the country by confiscating the vast majority of these estates and giving them to his own followers as a reward for their services, although a small number of existing landowners who accepted William were allowed to retain their property.

The area that is now Derbyshire was divided largely between the king and 15 favoured men, the rest being shared by the king's thanes, who were mainly of Saxon origin. A thane was a man who held property because of his military or other service to the king. As a local example, Elfin of Brailsford retained his manor. Of those favoured by William, Henry de Ferrers received well over a hundred manors, by far the largest share of the county. The new landowners in turn let land to subordinates who again often sub-let until in some cases the actual tenant of the land was a long way removed from the superior lord.

Most of this we know from the Domesday Book, which in spite of some inaccuracies, gives a fair idea of the size and importance of each town and village, the number of its inhabitants and its value. In many instances the previous dispossessed owner is also named. It is therefore from this book that we get our first detailed knowledge of Markeaton, which has two entries, and Mackworth, which has one.

Land belonging to Earl Hugh

In MARKEATON, Earl Siward had 9 carucates and a ½ of land taxable. Land for 9 ploughs. Earl Hugh has there 2 ploughs in Lordship; and 15 villeins and 7 bordars have 5 ploughs. There is a priest and a church, and 1 mill worth 6 shillings and 8 pence and 1 fishery and 24 acres of meadow. Woodland pasture 1 league long and ½ a league in breadth. Value before 1066 £4; now £3.

In the outliers of KNIVETON, MACKWORTH and ALLESTREE are 4 carucates of land taxable. Land for 4 ploughs. It is waste. There are 30 acres of meadow; and woodland pasture 1 league long and ½ a league in breadth. 1 carucate of these 4 is in EDNASTON, a manor of Henry's. Jocelyn holds it from the Earl and Colle pays Jocelyn 10 shillings and 8 pence from it.

Extract from Domesday Book showing the holdings of Earl Hugh Lupus of Chester in Markeaton, Mackworth and Allestree.

Land belonging to Henry de Ferrers

In MARKEATON, Aldith had 4 carucates of land taxable. Land for 4 ploughs. There are in Lordship 2 ploughs and 18 villeins and 5 bordars have 3 ploughs. There are 12 acres of meadow and woodland pasture 1 league long and 1 league in breadth. Value before 1066 and now 60 shillings.

Before going any further it would, perhaps, be useful to explain some of the terminology used in the Domesday entries. The carucate was a Danish area based on the English hide and reckoned as 120 acres or the land which could be ploughed by eight oxen, but this figure could vary locally and also according to the quality of the soil. The carucate could be divided into four virgates or eight bovates. The league was a unit of length, again flexible, and rated in this instance as about a mile and a half, although the author has a dictionary which specifies four versions extending to over three miles. Villeins and bordars were peasant farmers who, in spite of being poor, were nonetheless graded into degrees of poverty. Villeins were the highest ranking and held the most land, while below them came the bordars and, even lower, the cottars, who must have existed at the lowest possible level. The status of these classes was actually so low that there are recorded cases of land being sold or given and the occupants being included in the transaction and left to the mercy of their new owners. There are also slaves mentioned in Domesday and of these some could have been educated men employed for their academic skills and possibly enjoying a far better standard of living than the peasants.

The first thing we learn from the Domesday entries is that Markeaton was already divided into two manors held by Siward and Aldith. This comes as no great surprise as it was not an uncommon situation and the previous era was a period when much land changed hands forcibly as well as by peaceful means. It is also possible that it had been divided between two sons or perhaps passed by the marriage of daughters to other families. Siward was in fact Earl Siward of Northumbria and it has long been believed that it was he who was dispossessed by William for his part in the Ely rebellion of 1071, along with Hereward, Edwin and Morcar. However, more recent research has shown that he had died in 1055 and that his Markeaton holdings had passed to his heirs; the Siward who died at Ely was Siward Barn, who held land elsewhere in the county. Earl Siward had owned the part of the estate that contained what was later the main village, including the hall, church and mill, as well as the majority of the land. The rest of the manor, apparently consisting of outlying farms, was owned by Aldith, a woman of whom nothing now seems to be known apart from her brief mention in the Domesday Book. She may have been an heiress or a widow; either way, regardless of her situation, she was dispossessed by King William.

Aldith's lands went to Henry de Ferrers to swell his large holdings in this area, while Siward's portion was given, along with Mackworth, Allestree and Kniveton, to Hugh Lupus, the first Earl of Chester. There is some doubt as to whether the spelling of Chenivetun in Domesday really relates to Kniveton to the north-east of Ashbourne, and it is considered by some people to be another village, now lost, called Chevinton, perhaps taking its name from The Chevin a little to the north of Duffield. This theory requires the transposition of the letters 'n' and 'v' and one has to wonder why they were not in that order in the first place if the word really is intended to be Chevinton. If we accept the pronunciation of the 'Ch' in Cheniveton as being hard as in 'chorus' then Kniveton does seem to be a reasonable transcription from Domesday, taking into account the fact that most spelling over hundreds of years was phonetic. In any case, it may not really be so odd to have a relatively distant place like Kniveton as part of the manor, as people did own parcels of land in many various places and, even in the Domesday entry, one carucate of land lay in the manor of Ednaston some eight miles away. These separate parcels of land are known as 'discrete' manors and are not yet properly understood. A study of the discrete manor of Amesbury in County Wiltshire which was held by the Abbot there shows that all the outlying properties were also Roman sites, villas, farmsteads and so on, with very ancient place names and evidence of continuity of settlement.

Using this and similar evidence from elsewhere it is considered that the manor plus the outliers may represent elements of a Roman rural estate taken over completely by the Saxons and surviving into the Norman period. If this theory is right (and we may never be sure of the truth) then the manor of Markeaton with Kniveton and Ednaston could be one of these discrete manors and may therefore have very ancient origins indeed. Kniveton certainly is ancient, as it contains remains from the Neolithic to the post-mediaeval periods, including Saxon burials. Another possible example of this kind is Mickleover, which was held by the Abbot of Burton and which included the outliers of Findern and Potlock. Unfortunately both Kniveton and Ednaston disappear from the record after 1086 as far as being part of the manor of Markeaton is concerned, and we have to assume that they were probably sold soon after that date.

According to Domesday, the earl (Hugh d'Avranches, Earl of Chester) let the outliers of Mackworth, Allestree and Kniveton to one Gozelin or Jocelyn (son of Anketil de Touchet, a man of Norman birth) who was probably an officer or steward in the earl's service. By 1086 Jocelyn was already sub-letting some of the land in his care to a man called Colle, possibly a native Englishman, for the sum of 10s 8d. In spite of the implied notion that Jocelyn only held the outliers we can safely assume that where Domesday says 'Jocelyn holds it from the Earl', the 'it' referred to is the whole manor. This assumption is based on two facts: first that Earl Hugh must have had someone to run the Markeaton estate, although no one is specifically named and, secondly, that some years later Jocelyn's grandson, Henry de Touchet, became the owner of the manor. This information is contained in a charter of Earl Ranulph II of Chester dating from the period 1144–1149, which confirmed to Henry, son of Henry, son of Jocelyn, 'the whole of his land'. The de Touchets held the manor until 1497 or possibly 1516, but of this matter more will be said later. As we have no records of the precise area of Markeaton in those early days we do not know if the de Touchet manor included that part which belonged to Henry de Ferrers or whether this was absorbed into another of Henry's holdings.

If we read the Domesday entries for Markeaton and the outliers, the impression is given of a large thriving settlement with well over a thousand acres of arable land, grazing land and woodland, from which would come supplies of timber. It had its own mill and fishponds for food and was, by contemporary standards, a fairly well endowed estate. By contrast the outliers seem to have been uninhabited wasteland, without even a single plough for cultivation. This could have been the result of William's policy in the north of burning, destroying and killing virtually everything and everybody in order to render the land useless to invaders or other potential usurpers. For him this was cheaper and more effective than defending and fighting off any threatened takeover in that area. This *may* explain why there were no inhabitants recorded at Mackworth and why no value was put on the land, but if that was the case we have to wonder why Markeaton was allowed to continue as a thriving estate and why two other apparently useless tracts of land were given to a man so highly in favour as Henry de Ferrers. Deliberate destruction does seem doubtful and we are left with one of those odd situations to which we currently have no answer. Certainly the recovery of the land must have been well on the way or Jocelyn would not have been sub-letting to Colle for the then substantial sum of 10s 8d. (Compare this with the value of that very important item, the mill, which was rated at only 6s 8d.) This would not necessarily have been paid in cash, but most likely by giving service to Jocelyn.

As to the apparent absence of dwellings in the outliers, Domesday is not always accurate and some places, now believed to have existed in 1086, get no mention at all. There is also good reason to argue that there must have been a village of sorts at Allestree. The very name indicates that well before 1086 a man of some local power and authority, named Adelard or Athelard, associated himself with a particular tree, presumably because of its great age or size, which was possibly used as the village meeting place. Whether the great and undoubtedly ancient yew in the churchyard is that same tree is a question that will be argued over for a long time to come, but fortunately the elusive answer does not concern us here. In his book *Allestree, from Adelard to Raphael* J.W. Allen discusses this subject in more detail.

CHAPTER TWO

The Lords of the Manor

The Touchets

The correct pronunciation of this name is not certain. A commonly used version is spoken as Too-shay, as it would be in modern French, leaving the final T silent, and in 1318 Edmund Touscher was rector of Mackworth. However, with that one notable exception, it is a fact that through a very long period when English was mainly spelt phonetically, with virtually as many variations of a word as there were writers, this name has consistently retained the final T, which indicates that it was always pronounced.

The Touchets were the first family, of whom we have any positive knowledge, to own the manor and we are fortunate that the lineage can be traced with reasonable certainty to the earliest days after the Conquest. During the 400 years they were at Markeaton the family tree spread very wide and we shall therefore only consider those few of whom anything of direct interest is known. Those who went into the church are all mentioned in the section on Markeaton Church and the list of incumbents (see *Mackworth Church*) and need not concern us at this point.

From being stewards to the Earl of Chester in 1086 they had risen in status to owning the estate by the middle of the next century when Henry, Jocelyn's grandson, acquired the manor. They were definitely a family who, both socially and politically, were in the ascendant. The first one of possible passing interest is therefore Ranulf, second son of Jocelyn, who may have been Sheriff of Derby, but there is no evidence that he and the Ranulf mentioned later in the section on the church are one and the same person. The first Touchet of definite note is Thomas, who died in 1235. He was the first of the family to be knighted, an honour not to be repeated for four generations until Sir Robert, born in 1265, also earned the title. He was the father of Thomas Touchet, who is probably the one recorded as 'distressing the people of Ashbourne at the ford'. What he did on that occasion we may never know, but details of this sort, while certainly interesting, may also be misleading, and only go some of the way toward showing us what kind of people they were in those distant days. As it is we can only guess at the truth and it may be that, by so doing, we do them an injustice. We often get an impression of manorial lords as being very hard, unfeeling men, and some of them certainly were, but life itself was very hard by our standards and expectations at all levels were different to ours. They surely could not have all been bad squires who cared little for their people but, of course, there is no record of anything they may have done to ease the lot of their tenants. Only the bad bits seem to get into the record. This last Thomas was the father of Sir John, who married Joan, sister and heiress of Nicholas, fifth Lord Audley of Heleigh Castle, Cheshire. On the death of Nicholas in 1392 Sir John, through his wife, became the sixth Lord Audley.

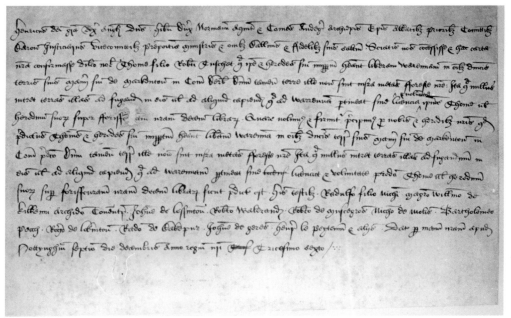

Copy of a document dated 1252 granting the right of free warren to Thomas Touchet. *(Derby Local Studies Library)*

His son, also Sir John, must have predeceased him as he never bore the title and it was, in turn, his son, again John, who became the seventh Lord Audley. He apparently died young in 1409, the same year as his great uncle Thomas who was rector of Mackworth. The Revd Thomas is an interesting anomaly in that, although the eldest son, he went into the church and the estate passed to his younger brother. The eighth Lord, James de Touchet, was Chief Justice for South Wales and was slain at Blore Heath while fighting for his king, Henry VI (1422–1461). His son John also held high office, being joint Commander-in-Chief of the army for Edward IV (1461–1483) and Lord Treasurer of England in 1484. He fought as a Yorkist at the battle of Bosworth in 1485 but was later pardoned. In 1468 he was

Engraved brass memorial of *c.*1525 to Sir Thomas Towchet, who died in 1490 at Shere in Surrey. His lower half was stolen prior to 1804 but has since been replaced. *(History and Antiquities of the County of Surrey, 1804)*

granted the manor of Shere in Surrey and a brass memorial to him in the church there is probably the only known likeness of any of the family. He died in 1490.

This John's son, James, 10th Lord Audley, was possibly the last of the line to be the absolute owner of Markeaton as he became involved in an unsuccessful insurrection of Cornishmen against Henry VII (1485–1509) which ended in their defeat at Blackheath in Kent on 17 June 1497. For this he was executed and attainted, which meant that his estates were confiscated by the Crown and other civil rights withdrawn, while the advowson of the church passed to the Abbot of Darley Abbey, who installed a vicar at Mackworth. Quite what happened during the interregnum we do not know, as the first recorded vicar was not installed until 1509. James left two sons, one of whom, John, became the 11th Lord Audley in 1512 on the restoration of the title by Henry VIII (1509–1547). He was granted repossession of Markeaton but he did not get the advowson of the church nor the manor of Shere, which returned to the Ormond family. Also, as will be seen shortly, there may have been financial difficulties as he sold Markeaton soon after.

The family moved to Ireland where they gradually recovered their wealth and status and in 1616 acquired the Earldom of Castlehaven. The Barony of Audley existed until the death of the 18th Lord Audley in 1777 when the line became extinct. James of Markeaton was, in fact, not the last Touchet to lose his head on the scaffold as, on 14 May 1631, Mervyn, second Earl of Castlehaven, was executed for committing practically every depraved and obscene crime imaginable. Perhaps Markeaton was well rid of this family.

It may be worthwhile explaining here that there is some confusion in the numbering of the Audley peerages. Current practice is to allot a number to the holder of a Barony only if that holder has actually received a Writ of Summons to the House of Lords. Thus James de Touchet, 10th Lord Audley, is in some reports only the seventh Baron to hold the title.

THE de TOUCHET-AUDLEY FAMILY.

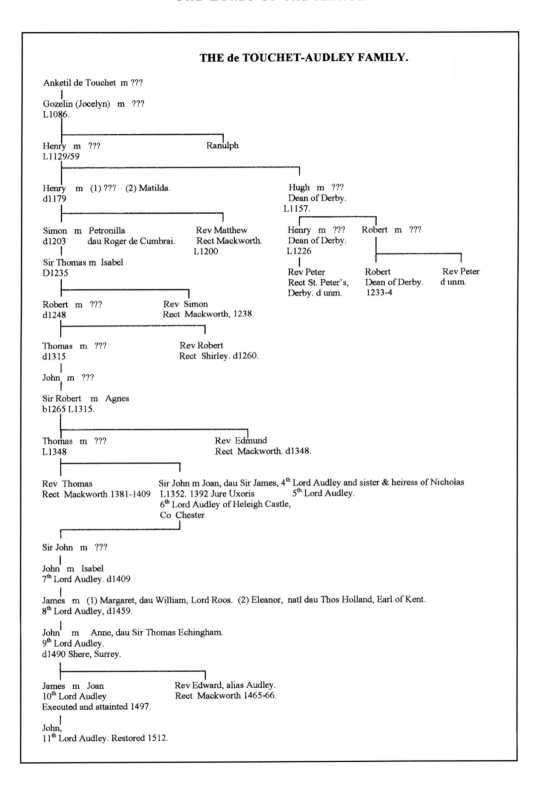

Anketil de Touchet m ???

Gozelin (Jocelyn) m ???
L1086.

Henry m ???   Ranulph
L1129/59

Henry   m (1) ???   (2) Matilda.   Hugh m ???
d1179   Dean of Derby.
                                           L1157.

Simon m Petronilla   Rev Matthew   Henry m ???   Robert m ???
d1203   dau Roger de Cumbrai. Rect Mackworth. Dean of Derby.
                          L1200   L1226

Sir Thomas m Isabel   Rev Peter   Robert   Rev Peter
D1235   Rect St. Peter's, Dean of Derby. d unm.
                                           Derby. d unm.   1233-4

Robert m ???   Rev Simon
d1248   Rect Mackworth, 1238.

Thomas m ???   Rev Robert
d1315   Rect Shirley. d1260.

John m ???

Sir Robert m Agnes
b1265 L1315.

Thomas m ???   Rev Edmund
L1348   Rect Mackworth. d1348.

Rev Thomas   Sir John m Joan, dau Sir James, 4th Lord Audley and sister & heiress of Nicholas
Rect Mackworth 1381-1409 L1352. 1392 Jure Uxoris   5th Lord Audley.
                          6th Lord Audley of Heleigh Castle,
                          Co Chester.

Sir John m ???

John m Isabel
7th Lord Audley. d1409

James m (1) Margaret, dau William, Lord Roos. (2) Eleanor, natl dau Thos Holland, Earl of Kent.
8th Lord Audley, d1459.

John   m   Anne, dau Sir Thomas Echingham.
9th Lord Audley.
d1490 Shere, Surrey.

James m Joan   Rev Edward, alias Audley.
10th Lord Audley   Rect Mackworth 1465-66.
Executed and attainted 1497.

John,
11th Lord Audley. Restored 1512.

The Mundy family

In common with many other old families the origins of the Mundys are not clear, but William was Mayor of High Wycombe, Buckinghamshire, during the reign of Henry VII (1485–1509) and there were family connections in Derbyshire via the Eyres of Hope in the early 14th century. In 1446 a Robert Mundy was returned to Parliament as a burgess for Derby. The derivation of the name Mundy has two versions, although one of them has a very dubious pedigree, having been reputedly created purely for status. This states that the family were of Mondai in France and that they came over with William the Conqueror. The other version is that in the days when surnames were still a rarity the peasants had to work one day a week for their lord. In this instance they worked Mondays and so became known as the Monday people, from which title the lord, in turn, took his, but the truth or otherwise of this story is lost in the past.

William Mundy had a son John, apparently an ambitious man who was a goldsmith and became Sheriff of London in 1514. He obviously desired the outward signs of status due to a successful businessman and to this end he became a country gentleman and squire by acquiring the Manor of Markeaton with Mackworth and Allestree in 1516. There may be some doubt about him getting the advowson of the church at this time as there is a record of the church being returned to the estate on the closure of Darley Abbey in 1536. Regrettably the truth of this situation is lost to us as many of the surviving Mundy papers were destroyed when Derby was flooded in May 1932.

There have, for many years, been three possible versions of how John came to acquire Markeaton from the reinstated Lord Audley: purchase, foreclosure and recovery. Of these only one had, until recently, contemporaneous documentary support, while at the same time being the most mysterious in that the circumstances surrounding it are not revealed. This document purports to be a deed of 23 November 1516 which concerns the recovery of the three manors with all their appurtenances and the advowson of Mackworth church by John Mundy from one William Goche. Who William Goche was and how he came to hold the estate after it had been confiscated by the Crown and reputedly returned to the Audleys are just two more items of interest on which we may never throw much light.

However, the recently found Markeaton Document, which is full of legal terminology, seems to partially clarify the matter. From it we learn that the reinstated Lord Audley '...*in Derby... first by Indenture of Bargain and Sale, secondly by Deed of Feofment* (granting of possession) *thereupon, thirdly by Fine and Recovery and fourthly by virtue of an order of the Lords of the Council in the Starchamber, did convey and assure the same manors unto Sir John Mundy, Knight, then Alderman of the City of London...*' From this it is clear that John Mundy purchased the manor from Lord Audley, although there seems to be an element of recovery of an unpaid debt or loan. There is an error in this account, written many years after the event, in that John Mundy had not been knighted at the time of the purchase. What is not mentioned anywhere is the advowson of the church, which does not seem to have been included in the deal. Perhaps this is where the enigmatic William Goche comes in, but see under *Mackworth Church*, page 126.

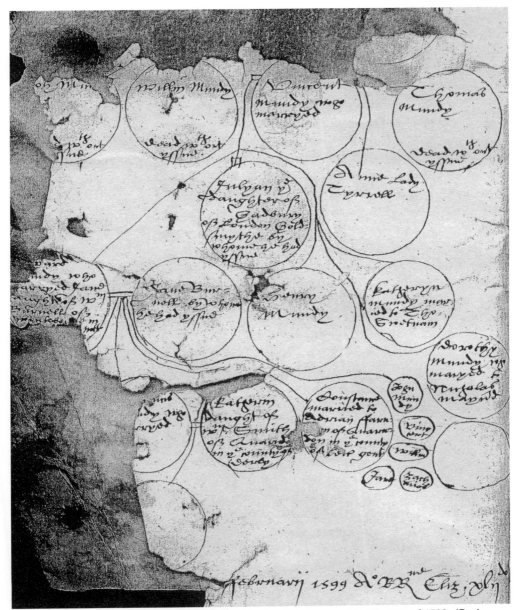

The beginning of the Markeaton Document, showing the damaged family tree of 1599. *(Derby Local Studies Library)*

John Mundy became Lord Mayor of London in 1522 and was knighted in 1529. He was married twice, his second wife being Juliana Browne, daughter of William Browne of Stretton-le-Fields in Derbyshire, who was himself twice Lord Mayor of London. On his death in 1537, Sir John's eldest son, Vincent, succeeded him at Markeaton and two other sons moved to Cornwall, where there were already old family connections, Thomas becoming Prior of Bodmin in 1540. Vincent, who became an MP and a JP, married Juliana Gadbury but left Markeaton when he became estranged from her. He it was who made the detailed inventory of the hall which is mentioned later under *Markeaton Hall*. The inventory is a fascinating record but the previously unanswered question, which has always hovered in the background, is 'Why did he write it?'

Here again the Markeaton Document gives a graphic insight into the situation: *'The said Vincent Mundy after the death of his father and loss of his said office by purchasing of the premises, liberall housekeeping, suertyship* (standing surety) *for others and by other like means became greatly indebted to other men so much that the revenues of the manors of Alstonfield, Warslow and Longnor in the county of Stafford nor of the said manor of Markeaton and premises in Derbyshire were not of sufficiency to clear his due debts for the payment whereof he was compelled to enter into divers statutes and to acknowledge many recognisances in the chancery. Of the which many remain there uncancelled although the remains of all these debts since his death have been paid by the said Edward Mundy his son.'* We now know that Vincent was not good at handling money and that the inventory of 1545 was made (presumably one for each manor) to assess his assets when he was in serious debt. He lived in this state for 26 years before reputedly being murdered in 1571 by a son, but reports differ as to whether the crime was committed by Henry or

Vincent junior, the latter being usually credited with the deed. It is notable that Vincent senior had written his will only a very short time prior to his death at the age of 61. Was there a connection?

On this subject the document again throws some light, although the paragraph is damaged and incomplete. It refers to '...*Edward Mundy elder son of the said Vincent for securing the said Edward to be indicted in the Kings bench as accessory unto Henry Mundy of the death of the said Vincent Mundy their father.'* In the absence of any mention of Vincent junior this leads us to believe the killer is possibly Henry. The outcome of this situation

FRANCISCVS MUNDY
de Markeaton in agro Derbiensi
Ætat: 29. Obijt Feb: 29. 1720.
Cunctis ille bonis flebilis occidit.

Francis Mundy (1690–1720), father of Wrightson who succeeded to the manor at the age of seven. *(Derby Local Studies Library)*

Bust of Francis Noel by Chantrey. Currently in the County Hall. *(Derby Local Studies Library)*

is not known, but certainly Edward came out of it in the clear as he inherited the estate and eventually paid off his father's debts. His tomb stands in Mackworth church.

The next eight generations produced several High Sheriffs and an MP, as well as intermarriage with other local families such as the Poles of Radbourne and the Cokes of Trusley. In 1677 Adrian Mundy bequeathed to the poor of Mark-eaton, Mackworth, Allestree,

Francis Noel Clark Mundy (1739–1815) with his grandson William. Engraved from a painting by R.R. Reinagle, 1809. This inspired Francis to write a poem to the artist. *(Private collection)*

Elizabeth, daughter of Sir Robert Burdett of Foremark, second wife of Francis Noel and mother of Francis and Charles. *(Derby Local Studies Library)*

Quarndon and Radbourne, 'to each town 20 shillings annually for ever'. The year 1715 saw the birth of Wrightson Mundy, son of Francis and Ann Noel. He was to become High Sheriff of Derbyshire in 1737 and an MP for Leicestershire in 1747. He was active in his support for the Jacobite cause and was one of the local men who met Prince Charles Edward Stuart at Radbourne Hall, the home of German Pole, in December 1745 when the Prince's army reached Derby on its ill-fated march to London.

What Wrightson could not possibly have known as he sat in that historic conference was that somewhere in that rabble army was a certain Captain William Maxwell, whose descendants would one day, on the extinction of the Mundy line, inherit the very manor through which he marched so hopefully on his way into Derby. And out again two days later! Wrightson was also responsible for the building of the last Markeaton Hall in 1755. He died in 1767.

Boy Archers by Joseph Wright, mid-1780s. Charles and Francis Mundy, sons of Francis Noel and Elizabeth. *(Private collection)*

Sarah Mundy (née Newton), wife of Francis, with their daughter Constance c.1814–15. From a miniature by F. Cruikshank. *(Private collection)*

Photograph of William Mundy (1801–1877). *(Derby Local Studies Library)*

Harriot Georgiana Mundy (née Frampton, *d*.1886), wife of William. From a watercolour by Guido Bach, 1863. *(Private collection)*

Carte de Visite of Francis Noel Mundy (1833–1903), the last Mundy to live at Markeaton. *(Derby Local Studies Library)*

Carte de Visite of Emily Georgiana Mundy (*c*.1846–1929), wife of Francis Noel. *(Derby Local Studies Library)*

Three generations later, on 20 December 1832, Constance, daughter of Francis Mundy, married William Henry Fox-Talbot, a scientist, of Lacock Abbey in Wiltshire. During a tour of Derbyshire and Yorkshire he had stayed for a while at Markeaton, from where he wrote to his stepfather on 7 November 1832 '...I am going to be married, the object of my choice is Constance, youngest daughter of Mr Mundy of Markeaton'. Constance was a talented artist who encouraged her new husband to draw and paint, but for all his desire to emulate her he was unable to satisfactorily put on paper what he saw before him.

To overcome what he saw as an annoying disability he turned his scientific mind to other ways of creating pictures and to this end he devoted much of his life to the development of photography. He is rightly famous for the pioneering work he did in this field, becoming known in this country as the 'Father of Photography', although it has to be acknowledged that in Europe a number of scientists were also working successfully to make use of the then

Constance (1811–1880), daughter of Francis and Sarah Mundy and wife of William Henry Fox Talbot. Carte de Visite. *(Private collection)*

William Henry Fox Talbot of Lacock Abbey, Wiltshire. *(Derby Local Studies Library)*

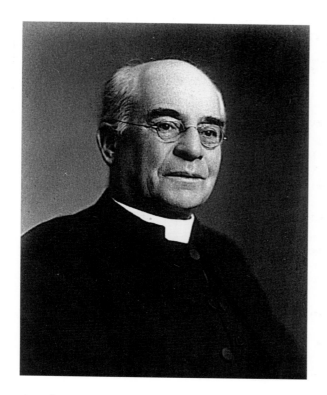

Revd Prebendary William Gilchrist
Clark-Maxwell (1865–1935).
Succeeded to the estate in 1929.
(Private collection)

recently discovered light sensitive properties of certain silver salts and between them inventing several workable processes. However, out of all these, Fox-Talbot was the first to create a negative from which multiple positive images could be made, and this principle is still the basis of modern photography. In spite of Fox-Talbot's achievements and his family connections there is no record of his ever taking any photographs locally, although he did send some specimens of his early work to Constance's sister Laura, who was delighted with them but later disappointed when they faded; at that time the means of permanently fixing images had yet to be discovered.

The last Mundy to live at Markeaton was Francis Noel, who died in 1903. On his widow's death in 1929 the estate passed to his cousin, the Reverend Prebendary William Gilchrist Clark-Maxwell. When he in turn died in 1935 his two sons inherited, the first time the lordship had been divided for at least eight centuries. Between 1929 and 1934 the hall and park were sold to the Borough of Derby. The rest of the estate remains with the family to this day, although it is currently divided between the Revd W.G. Clark-Maxwell's three grandchildren. After World War Two two large areas were acquired for building purposes and the Mackworth and Markeaton estates were laid out, although the latter has long since been considered to be part of Allestree.

More information concerning the last lady of the manor, Emily Mundy, can be found in the final chapter, *Varieties*.

THE MUNDY FAMILY.

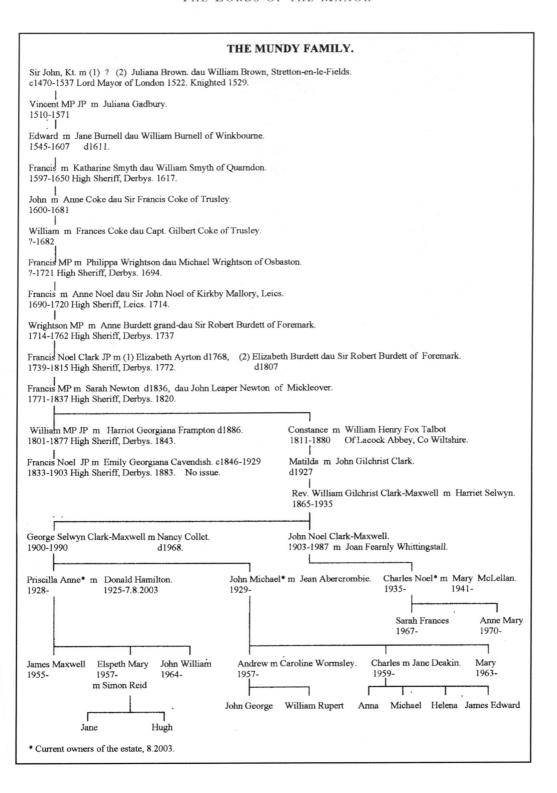

Sir John, Kt. m (1) ? (2) Juliana Brown. dau William Brown, Stretton-en-le-Fields.
c1470-1537 Lord Mayor of London 1522. Knighted 1529.

Vincent MP JP m Juliana Gadbury.
1510-1571

Edward m Jane Burnell dau William Burnell of Winkbourne.
1545-1607   d1611.

Francis m Katharine Smyth dau William Smyth of Quarndon.
1597-1650 High Sheriff, Derbys. 1617.

John m Anne Coke dau Sir Francis Coke of Trusley.
1600-1681

William m Frances Coke dau Capt. Gilbert Coke of Trusley.
?-1682

Francis MP m Philippa Wrightson dau Michael Wrightson of Osbaston.
?-1721 High Sheriff, Derbys. 1694.

Francis m Anne Noel dau Sir John Noel of Kirkby Mallory, Leics.
1690-1720 High Sheriff, Leics. 1714.

Wrightson MP m Anne Burdett grand-dau Sir Robert Burdett of Foremark.
1714-1762 High Sheriff, Derbys. 1737

Francis Noel Clark JP m (1) Elizabeth Ayrton d1768,   (2) Elizabeth Burdett dau Sir Robert Burdett of Foremark.
1739-1815 High Sheriff, Derbys. 1772.   d1807

Francis MP m Sarah Newton d1836, dau John Leaper Newton of Mickleover.
1771-1837 High Sheriff, Derbys. 1820.

William MP JP m Harriot Georgiana Frampton d1886.   Constance m William Henry Fox Talbot
1801-1877 High Sheriff, Derbys. 1843.   1811-1880   Of Lacock Abbey, Co Wiltshire.

Francis Noel JP m Emily Georgiana Cavendish. c1846-1929   Matilda m John Gilchrist Clark.
1833-1903 High Sheriff, Derbys. 1883.   No issue.   d1927

                                          Rev. William Gilchrist Clark-Maxwell m Harriet Selwyn.
                                          1865-1935

George Selwyn Clark-Maxwell m Nancy Collet.   John Noel Clark-Maxwell.
1900-1990   d1968.   1903-1987 m Joan Fearnly Whittingstall.

Priscilla Anne* m Donald Hamilton.   John Michael* m Jean Abercrombie.   Charles Noel* m Mary McLellan.
1928-   1925-7.8.2003   1929-   1935-   1941-

                                                                      Sarah Frances   Anne Mary
                                                                      1967-   1970-

James Maxwell Elspeth Mary John William   Andrew m Caroline Wormsley.   Charles m Jane Deakin.   Mary
1955-   1957-   1964-   1957-   1959-   1963-
               m Simon Reid

                                            John George William Rupert   Anna Michael Helena James Edward
        Jane   Hugh

* Current owners of the estate, 8.2003.

CHAPTER THREE

Markeaton Village

WHAT WAS Markeaton like in the 11th century? The hall and church would probably have stood fairly close together, with the mill sited on the brook nearby. There could also have been a house for the priest, which may have been built directly onto the church. Whether there ever was a church actually in Markeaton will be discussed later. Until recent years it was believed that the peasants' houses would have been clustered around the hall and church in what has long been accepted as a typical layout for an early mediaeval village. Such a village would have been composed of crude, timber-framed, single-roomed huts, the walls of which were infilled with wattle and a mixture of animal dung and clay and the roofs thatched with straw or reeds. Excavations at various sites in the country have shown the lifespan of this type of hovel to be about 20 years, after which time they would have been so dilapidated that rebuilding would be necessary. Each hovel would have stood in its own toft, or yard, in which vegetables, fruit and herbs could be grown and livestock overwintered. However, evidence is emerging from around the country to show that this concept of the nucleated early mediaeval village is probably inaccurate. Many of these so-called villages actually consisted of widely scattered, single farmsteads and this idea is already implied by the two Domesday entries for Markeaton.

How else do we explain the fact that Siward, while holding the church and mill, had fewer people on his share of the land than Aldith? This means that there was probably no nucleated village as such until sometime after the Domesday survey (hence the previous use of the word settlement rather than village), and there was merely a grouping of those buildings that were important or profitable to the lord. The isolated smallholdings would have been tucked away on small plots of wasteland among the great areas of cultivation strips which were the prime feature of the agricultural system at that time. A group of strips was known as a furlong, a word that has no connection with its modern counterpart of one eighth of a mile. Each peasant farmer would have rented, or even occasionally owned, a number of these strips, which were scattered across the estate and on which he grew his own food. This was done in close collaboration with the other tenant farmers, for the sake of crop rotation, with whom he also shared the common grazing land.

When the land later returned to pasture the strips were fossilised and there are many good examples locally, of which the best one for public access is the Markeaton pitch and putt course. This area can be seen on the map below as a group of plots to the south-west of Markeaton village. Even today their boundary ditches can be traced on the ground and from the air. Ridge (or rig) and furrow fields were created by the plough being used in such a way that it always turned the earth in toward the centre of the strip and thus, gradually, the ridged plot was formed.

This system continued in use for hundreds of years until landowners discovered the profitability of rearing stock, which required less effort and fewer people to do the work, although some arable land was retained for the necessary crops. This was a miserable time for many of the peasantry who, owning nothing and having no rights, suddenly found themselves evicted and left homeless and unwanted to make way for sheep and cattle.

The early hall would have been larger and better built than the peasants' houses, but even so it probably consisted of little more than one large room, hence its title, the Hall. The church, wherever it stood, may have been of timber or stone, as there are traces of Saxon stonework in a number of fairly local churches, the best examples being those at Stanton-by-Bridge and, of course, Repton. The stone foundations of the Saxon minster church of St

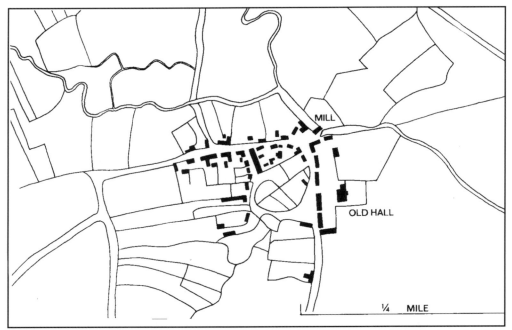

Map. Enlarged detail section from the map showing the size of Markeaton Village in the mid-18th century and the roads and streams. Sometime before 1836 this village was reduced to the small hamlet which now stands by the west gate of Markeaton Park.

Markeaton Park and village showing areas of mediaeval ridge and furrow. The 1930s lake runs diagonally across the right-hand side with the hall site, gardens and village about centre. Markeaton Lane runs diagonally from centre to bottom left where it meets Ashbourne Road. *(Derbyshire County Council Survey, 1971)*

Alkmund in Derby were found in 1968 but were then destroyed in the name of urban development. The site of the third important building, the mill, will also be mentioned later.

Gradually, Jocelyn and his successors grew in wealth and status and in 1330 the Touchets claimed a park and a gallows for the execution of criminals. This last item implies that they had the right to try and convict those brought before them, which shows just how much power these feudal lords had over the lower classes. How many unfortunates, if any, were hanged locally we have no means of knowing.

Many years later emparking came to be dreaded by the villagers as for many of them it meant removal to a new place outside the park boundary (if they were lucky) or, worse still, plain eviction (if they were unlucky). One example of this occurred at Castle Howard in Yorkshire, where three villages were cleared without any provision whatever for the inhabitants. Whether this happened at Markeaton seems doubtful, but the fact remains that in the mid-18th century the bulk of the village was inside the park to the west of the hall, as well as round the green just outside the west gate, where the remains of the village still stand. If we accept that some of the buildings indicated on the 18th-century map are in fact rows of cottages similar to those still standing at nearby Mackworth, then there were possibly as many as 30 to 40 families living within the park boundary. However, by 1836 the first edition of the OS 1-inch map shows only a handful of buildings other than the hall within the park and one of these can possibly be identified as the Dower House, which stood by the north-west corner of the hall complex.

Another building shown on the OS map may be the old mill house, but on such a small scale it is very difficult to be sure and in any case it may have been an integral part of the mill. What is certain is that between the production of those two maps the village within the park dwindled from 30 to 40 houses to no more than five. When and why did this happen and where did the villagers go? The answer to 'when?' is probably about the time the hall was rebuilt in around 1755. As for why, Wrightson Mundy, having built his fashionable new hall, needed to surround it with an equally fashionable park and this required the removal of the village. The landscaping of the 185-acre park was almost certainly done at the direction of William Emes (see *Varieties*), using the work of the nationally well-known Lancelot 'Capability' Brown as his inspiration.

The park claimed by the Touchets over 400 years earlier was purely utilitarian for the raising of deer and boar for hunting and was not laid out or landscaped. Its situation is commemorated in the names Park Farm and Park Fields, which were in an area to the north of Kedleston Road and from the latter, eventually, two large houses took their names. One of these later became a grammar school for girls. On removal of the school to the Mackworth Estate the name went too and it is now known as Parkfields Mackworth College.

The fashion of emparking which came later was a matter of displaying status and many new country houses were built in grand isolation, away from the common herd and surrounded by landscaped grounds. In those days it really was a case of 'you've either got it or you haven't.' The majority hadn't. To date no record of the removal of the village has been found, which is understandable, but it does leave us wondering what sort of landlords the Mundys were. Would they, like other landlords, have had the temperament to evict their tenants and demolish the village without replacement? A century earlier the answer would probably have been 'yes', as it is recorded that in 1654 John Mundy, 'a powerfull man', sequestrated the rents of certain fields at Allestree, thus preventing the church from claiming some of its rightful income. In spite of many protests his son William and his grandson Francis continued to hold those fields and they were still in Francis's hands at his death in 1720. His son, also Francis, died in the same year and it was therefore his son, Wrightson Mundy, who inherited the situation. What he did about the fields we do not know, but that he ordered the clearance of the village is not in doubt. This brings us to the third question: 'Where did the inhabitants go?'

In a village of that size there could have been upwards of 200 people, but we have to consider the possibility that the village had already dwindled and that a number of cottages were empty when the clearance came. There are so many known cases of eviction from around the country that any such event locally would surely have lived on in folk memory even if it was not actually recorded, and the total silence on the subject supports the argument that Wrightson Mundy did no such thing. Some tenants could have moved into nearby Derby or possibly Mackworth or Allestree. The probability is that most were rehoused in specially built cottages on plots of wasteland on the estate (of which the sites of several are known) and at least three new lodges were built around the park. Interestingly this virtually re-established the situation of the non-nucleated village we have already noted at the beginning of this chapter.

West entrance to Markeaton Park showing the peculiar arrangement of the Lodge and gatepost. Which came first? *(Author)*

Certainly by the end of the century all trace of the mediaeval village had vanished, as we are told that Catherine Hutton and her father William, the well-known 18th-century local historian, visited Markeaton hoping to find the house where his grandmother was born. They found a distant relative named Bennet and enquired the way: 'He took us into a little solitary croft, to which now not even a path pointed. "Here" says he "stood our house, there the public house and there our other neighbours". They were utterly gone and cattle grazing over the habitations of man and beast. I looked pensively round to mark the spot'. It is interesting to note the presence of a former place of refreshment, although that probably moved no further than to just outside the west gate. (see *Varieties*). It may have been the 'Cock', as that appeared in an advertisement in the *Derby Mercury* of 15 June 1764. In the early 1980s the remains of plaster floors were found in a farmyard near the park gate, which may have belonged to later mediaeval cottages. One of the present farm buildings stands on a stone base which almost certainly once supported a timber-framed building. Three substantial brick houses which stand in a row by the tiny green were built

Home Farm House, built *c.*1760. A very desirable dwelling for that period and today. Much of the internal timber came from the previous Markeaton Hall. *(Author)*

At left is a farmhouse in the village which formerly doubled as the village ale house, the Nimrod and Hotspur, until its closure in 1904. It also contains timber from the old hall. The small sloping roof was the brewhouse, since demolished, as was the farmhouse beyond it. On the right, across the road, is the Old Forge, the former smithy. Photo dated 1937.

The same house, attractively modernised, as seen in 1984. (Author)

House on The Green
that was originally
two cottages.
(Author)

The Old Forge
*c.*1690. *(Private
collection)*

Beamed ceiling in the Old Forge. *(Author)*

in around 1760 and contain much reused timber, including some very substantial beams, which without doubt came from the old hall, then recently replaced by Wrightson Mundy. Not that these were the first brick buildings in the village.

Across the road stands the former blacksmith's shop, now known as The Old Forge, which is over 300 years old, while much of the timber in it is older still. The wood in question is reused and reputedly came from old river barges being broken up at Swarkestone. While this may be fact in this instance, it has to be said that if it is true for every house making this claim then the river must at one time have been very busy indeed. Good timber was a valuable commodity and many houses were built with that which was carefully saved from demolished properties. As for the general situation here, whatever the truth may be, of one fact we can be certain, that Markeaton village all but vanished from the landscape it had occupied for at least 700 years.

Wall in the garden of the Old Forge constructed from the west front steps of Markeaton Hall, which was demolished in November 1964. (Author)

CHAPTER FOUR

Markeaton Church

OF ALL the gaps in our knowledge of the history of this manor the situation regarding the apparent disappearance of Markeaton Church is the most intriguing. We have seen that in 1086 Markeaton was the local centre of religion, having a church and a priest to administer to the spiritual needs of the manor. However, by the middle of the 12th century there are indications that a change was taking place. This is first hinted at in the *Cartulary of Darley Abbey*, in which there is a memorandum: 'That at an inquest made by the command of King Henry II [1154–1189], before Ranulph the Sheriff [a Touchet?], Froger Arch Deacon of Derby and Peter of Sandiacre, in the house of Hugh, Dean of Derby [a Touchet], the twenty-four recognitors affirmed on oath that the church of St Peter in Derby was founded and built on the patrimony of the said Hugh and his predecessors to whom the advowson of the said church belongs'.

The subject matter of this document does not concern us here (apart from the points of interest that certainly one, and possibly two, Touchets held positions of power in the town and that the family claims to have founded, or perhaps refounded, the church of St Peter, as there is a presumed record of it being held by one Leofric prior to 1066) but what is relevant is that two of the witnesses are named as Roger, priest of Markeaton and Robert, priest of Mackworth and that the date was sometime in 1156 or 1157.

Having given us this crumb of information, history then leaves us without a clue as to the prevailing situation at that time. Fortunately, about 40 years later, we are presented with another small but important item of knowledge. The Touchets had become benefactors of Darley Abbey and this second item, also from the *Cartulary*, is an extract from a grant of land to the Abbey dated simply to the late 12th century. It reads: '...by the grant of Matthew de Touchet parson of the Mother church of Mackworth and of Henry who holds the Chapel of Allestree from the Mother church of Mackworth...'. This tells us that the church was definitely established at Mackworth before the year 1200, as was the forerunner of the present church at Allestree. Spiritual matters then, as in many other manors, were firmly in the hands of the local lord and his family. The Touchets seem to have had a genuine interest in religion, not only for the good of their souls, for which they were generous in their gifts and leases of land (doubtless in return for a suitable amount of intercessionary prayer) but also for the undisputed power and control it gave them in local affairs.

To this end they were to provide several rectors at Mackworth over the next 300 years or so, although the line was not continuous, until 1497 when James unsuccessfully rebelled against King Henry VII (1485–1509) and as a result the patronage of the church passed to Darley Abbey. What happened to the then incumbent, the Revd Edward Somer, we do not know, but not until 1509 did the Abbot install a vicar at Mackworth. Other priests of the Touchet line were Hugh, Dean of Derby; Henry, Dean of Derby (Hugh's son); Peter, Rector of St Peter's, Derby (Hugh's grandson); Robert, Dean of Derby (his other grandson) and Robert, Rector of Shirley.

What of Markeaton Church? We are faced with three potential situations, for none of which, unfortunately, is there any historical evidence. The easiest to dispose of is the possibility that there were two churches and that, for some unknown reason, the one at Markeaton closed down, with the patronage being transferred to Mackworth. J.W. Allen, in his book *Allestree, from Adelard to Raphael,* suggests the possibility of a pre-Conquest chapel at Allestree and the argument holds good for Mackworth as well. Ten miles to the west Cubley had a church in 1086, while neighbouring Marston Montgomery is omitted from the record, yet it is in Marston church that we find Saxon remains in the form of the chancel arch and a window. The fact that Domesday makes no mention does not necessarily mean that there was previously nothing there, but we have to admit to having no record of any religious establishment in Mackworth pre-1200. The presence of the two priests may be a hint, and Robert may indeed be the first recorded incumbent of Mackworth, but we do not know this as a fact and it should not be allowed to confuse the issue or cause us to jump to wrong conclusions; he or Roger could simply have been resident in one of the villages for any number of reasons. Therefore, in the absence of evidence, this version must be put on one side as no more than a possibility.

The second potential situation is that there was a church at Markeaton and that it was moved to a new site at Mackworth. If there was originally a church actually in Markeaton village then we can assume it to have been defunct before the end of the 12th century, as there is no further mention of it or a priest after the reference in the *Darley Cartulary.* As to the question of why it should have been moved there is no answer that can be based on fact. All that can be said is that, as they already had control of the church, and the income from it, the move was a family decision by the Touchets and it was for the ultimate benefit of that family.

There is a theory that the church was placed roughly halfway between the manor houses of Markeaton and Mackworth for the convenience of both families. As the de Mackworths cannot be positively traced before the early 13th century, this idea lacks proof. It is nonetheless possible that the de Mackworths held the manor early enough for it to be a feasible theory. Certainly, as a family they seem to have found considerable favour with the Touchets. (see *The de Mackworth Family*).

We should also bear in mind the possibility of there being a chapel in Markeaton Hall by this time, as there was definitely one there later. By the early 15th century the de Mackworths also had a private chapel. A record dated 30 May 1408 tells us that the Bishop of Lichfield granted to Thomas Mackworth 'his licence to have an oratory in the house of his habitation within the Vill of Mackworth'.

Regardless of other factors the appointment of Matthew de Touchet, brother of the manorial lord, as incumbent gave him a potentially good personal income, as the rector (or ruler) of a parish claimed tithes of one-tenth of all local produce and income, which meant in theory that he could live in relative comfort and have plenty for himself while the peasants could be near starvation, especially after a bad harvest. Whether this actually happened depended largely on the ethics of the individual priest, but there were undoubtedly some bad cases where men used their position purely for personal gain and God came in a distant second. Hopefully, allowing that the Christian morals and human compassion of the de Touchet priests was of the highest order, they would still have been well off by contemporary standards. Of course the picture nationally was nowhere near so clear cut and there were also many priests, some locally, who were little, if any, better off than the peasants and who struggled to live.

If there was a separate church at Markeaton then its site is unknown and there is very little information relating to it. In the Derbyshire Archaeological Journal of 1889 there is a reference to stone remains in Markeaton said to be those of a church, but this article, like so many others, fails to state the geographical location of the site and there is no record of any such feature today.

When this investigation was initiated in 1986 a short length of wall was found built into a hedge near the Mackworth Brook, which was composed of stone blocks of various sizes up to five feet or more in length, on some of which there was evidence of moulding or carving. On the bank of the brook and in the water was more stone, again showing distinct signs of carving. Some of the blocks seemed to be quite old, but the carved ones were of no great age. More confusing was the fact that some stones bore obvious traces of paint, indicating that they had been removed from a building fairly recently. Fortunately, during the investigation of this apparent enigma, a chance meeting solved the problem. The wall was built for horse jumping and the stone came from the site of a large city centre store that had been erected some years earlier. As this stone (and brick hardcore) came by the lorry load it seems that the older blocks may have come from a previous building on the site and were excavated during clearance. Unfortunately we do not know which was the city store in question.

There was formerly a field, called Church Field (le Kyrke Field), in the manor and Dr J.C. Cox records this fact in his voluminous work, published in 1877, *The Churches of Derbyshire*. A note in this book gives the impression that the field still existed at that date and could be a clue to the site of the church, but unfortunately this is not so, as Church Field was one of the large open fields into which the manor was divided before the enclosures. It stretched from the line of the footpath between Markeaton Lane and Mackworth church to well south of Ashbourne Road, with its western boundary on the hedgerow immediately to the east of the church. A large scale map of 1864 confirms the fact that, by that date, the only field with even a hint of church in its name was Churchyard Close, and this still exists as the most westerly field in Markeaton and is adjacent to the field in which Mackworth church stands. It is therefore part of the original Church Field, from which it takes its name, and has nothing to do with the site of the presumed church at Markeaton.

This brings us to the third possibility, which is based on the premise that the church was not moved for the simple reason that it was always on or very near its present site (see Mackworth Church, p123). The fact that the name has changed is of no importance, as the name of the church could vary from time to time depending on the writer of any particular record and a print published as late as 1805, clearly depicting Mackworth Church in its pre-restoration condition, is labelled as Markeaton, Derby. If it was on its present site in 1086, Earl Hugh, the owner, would surely have claimed such an important feature as part of his capital messuage and had it included under Markeaton. Nor is the fact that the church is so far from Markeaton Hall unique, as the church isolated in the field between Brailsford and Ednaston has always served two villages, to the extent that in the Domesday Book each is credited with half a church. Regretfully, we must concede that the situation regarding this church is one of those that was not recorded and about which we will probably never know the truth.

CHAPTER FIVE

Markeaton Hall

IN THE early days at Markeaton the lord or head man would have lived in a timber-framed building, which was both better built and larger than those in which the peasants lived. As wealth and ambition increased so did the size of the hall and with it the status gulf between the lord and his tenants. As stone became more widely used for building purposes some became self-contained fortifications, castellated and moated, rather than simply dwelling houses. Many mediaeval manor houses were surrounded by a moat for protection, although some later ones seem to have had this feature purely as a status symbol. Exuperius Turner, the 18th-century squire of nearby Bearwardcote, is reputed to have kept a bear in his! The hall at Markeaton may originally have been moated but if this was the case then any sign of it has long since vanished.

Of the outward appearance of the hall the Touchets lived in we know nothing, and can only guess at a large timber and plaster house of the type which was then common and of which a few examples remain nationally. Locally a good later one is at Somersall Herbert. Nor do we do know when their hall at Markeaton was built, but John Mundy, arriving in 1516, seems to have rebuilt it not long after in the manner suited to a man destined to become Lord Mayor of London and a knight of the realm. His imposing new house had the main front facing west with the ground floor and basement built in stone, the central front door being approached by steps with a tiled canopy over. Above this was the timber-framed first floor, having 10 gables, and rising high over these was another storey, again in stone, six bays wide and surmounted by three more pointed gables and chimneys; in 1662 tax was paid on 11 hearths. A service wing adjoined to the north and there were formal gardens to the east and west with ornamental trees. The whole was enclosed by a stone wall. To the north and south of the western garden was an extensive range of outbuildings, again timber-framed on a buttressed stone plinth, some of which may have survived from the previous hall, for this was a working farm. In the centre of the western range was the arched main

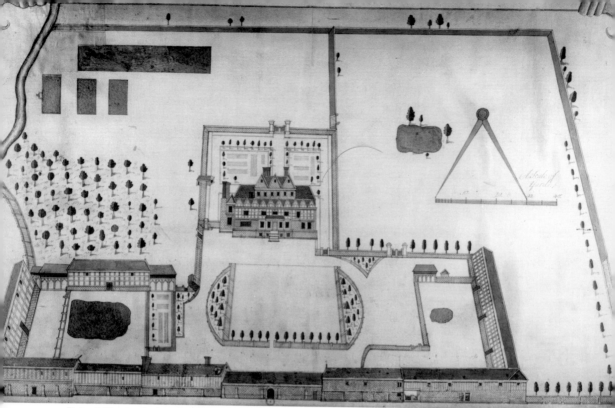

Robert Blanton's drawing of 1753 entitled 'East South-East Birdflight View of Markeaton Hall and Gardens near Derby'. This hall was built fairly soon after 1516 and taken down in 1755, some of the timber being reused in new houses in Markeaton Village. Note the pump in the yard to the left of the house. *(Derby Museum and Art Gallery)*

entrance to the complex as the road to the hall was a different one to the present Main Drive and entered the estate at the Side Gate off Ashbourne Road. (see *Roads*).

All this we know from a picture entitled 'East South East Birdflight View of Markeaton Hall and Gardens', drawn by Robert Blanton in 1753, only a couple of years before it was demolished. We must bear in mind the fact that, far from being a 'Birdflight View', the artist drew this from ground level, using his imagination for the aerial perspective. The picture shows us the hall and outbuildings in what seems to be quite accurate detail down to the water pump in the yard immediately to the left of the hall. At the end of the 18th century, William Hutton, the local historian, wrote '[At Markeaton] an old hall of timber and plaister was taken down about 40 years ago'. The building in the picture appears to belie

Detail from Blanton's drawing showing the buttress at the north-west angle of the outbuildings. This still stands. *(Derby Museum and Art Gallery)*

Hutton's description as we can see a lot of stone, but relatively little timber and plaster, but this is the grand front of the house and there would have been rather more timber in the rest of it. Certainly the interior would have been largely constructed of those materials. Outside the complex was a larger fenced enclosure, possibly for recreation, bounded on the north by the brook, which insulated the family home from the lower classes, for the rest of what we now know as the park was farmland in regular use. Within this enclosed area were fishponds and what may well have been an orchard. Leading into this outer area from the formal gardens were two gateways with ornate stone pillars and we may wonder if these are the ones which later graced the Ashbourne Road and Markeaton Lane entrances.

If the 'Scale of Yards' on the picture is reasonably accurate then the hall seems to have stood a few yards to the east of the site of its successor but, of course, the perspective of such a drawing may be deceptive and the 1740s map places it precisely where Wrightson Mundy's hall stood. The position of the farm complex we can establish quite accurately as parts of the stone-built plinth still exist on the north and west sides, having been deemed suitable as the base for the later range of stable buildings. At the extreme bottom left of the picture is a buttress and this still stands, with a blocked-up doorway close by in the north wall (see lower picture, p50). The original entrance would have been where the wide steps now lead to the terrace. The small circle on the picture just below the arched entrance is the mark left by a rusty drawing pin (!) which shows that this valuable document has not always been treated with the care and respect it now enjoys. The drawing may flatter the

Buttress and blocked doorway in the outbuildings of the old Markeaton Hall. *(Author)*

The modern toilet block is built directly onto the remains of the old hall outbuildings. *(Author)*

condition of a house two and a quarter centuries old, but the impression is given that it was finally removed because it had become unfashionable rather than dilapidated.

A final word on the picture. The artist can be forgiven all his technical faults except one, which must have been obvious even 250 years ago. The slight shadows on the top three gables show the sun to be high in the southern sky, while at the same time every tree in sight is lit from the north!

As well as the picture of Sir John Mundy's fine hall, we have some knowledge of the interior from the inventory which, as we have seen earlier, was made in 1545 by Vincent Mundy who, having inherited it on Sir John's death in 1537, became heavily indebted to numerous creditors. The inventory is in Vincent's own hand and as well as the contents of the house it includes such expendables as livestock, poultry and even (by God's grace) the estimated value of the crops in the fields. The contents of each room are given in detail from large items such as the oak table, six yards long, in the hall, down to the cooking pots in the kitchen. The hall had so many rooms containing beds one could be excused for thinking that it was an hotel being written about rather than a private house. The servants slept in a 'gret chamber' while the cook seems to have had sufficient rank to have qualified for a private room. Private is probably a word to be treated very warily as there would have been few, if any, corridors and one room would simply have led to another.

Apart from the normal rooms one would expect to find in a rambling country house there was also a chapel and an armoury. The latter was situated in 'the lytell buttery adjoining the upper hall'. The vestments and contents of the chapel are given in detail and include mass books and a psalter. There were very few of what we would call private possessions but among those in the study was a book *The Siege of Troy*. This was written in about 1420 by John Lydgate, a monk of Bury St Edmunds, for presentation to King Henry V (1412–1422). This copy was probably made for William Carent of Carent's Court, Isle of Purbeck, as there is a beautiful illumination of his arms at the end of the volume. John Mundy seems to have acquired it in about 1510 and in 1534 passed it to his son, Vincent, who, in 1545, valued it at 13s 4d. It was later in the possession of Adrian Mundy, followed by Francis Mundy in 1615. It then had several owners, eventually coming to Mrs Rylands, and it is now in the John Rylands Library in Manchester, where it has been described as 'a splendid specimen of 15th-century illumination'.

An extract from the inventory is included here with the glossary of obscure words found in it. The inventory can be seen in its entirety in the DAJ Vol. 51, 1930 and in the first edition of this book both of which are in the Derby Local Studies Library. The document has marginal notes as to the destination of the various items. Some are marked 'my wyff' or 'my w': others 'EM' (his son Edward) and others 'ex'; this last signifying that they were to be disposed of by his executors in partial payment of his debts.

```
                Inventorie of
                Marketon the sted
                      &c.
        Tot^lls to be of stuff only  lxxi^ll videlicet my wiff
          xx^ll ffor E.M. xxx^ll and to my ex^ors at Sted etc
          xx^ll
        cccxlv^ll xvij^s x^d
        ccciiij^xx viij^ll v^s
        The Cattell goyng at the sted. xvj
          Junii an. xxxvij h. viij                    (=1545)
ex.     Off oxen vj at iij^ll the yoke pic'                  ix^ll
ex.     Off mylche kye viij and j Bull at xvi^s
          the pece                                    vij^ll iiij^s
        Off Sterys ij at xij^s the pece  p'is             xxiiij^s
        Off Twynts  viij ^ll/iiij  oxen/iiij hey-
          ers/ at viijs                                iij^ll iiij^s
        Off Calves weynelyngs iiij at iiij^s              xvj^s
        It' j colt and iij yong mares at xx^s the
          pece viz: the rone fyle/the done fyle/
          Ratlyffs mares fyle and the colt              iiij^ll
        It' Se James Mares colt suckyng  p'is            xij^s
        It' the Lytell Mare, with her fole
          suckyng                                    xiij^s iiij^d
        It the olde Whyte gelding  pis                 xxiiij
        It the Curtall,  p'is                         xxiiij^s

        It' the Croppe of corne on the ground,
          viz. of Wheat of Rye of Drege  and
          of paese, to be worth by Gods grace
          by estmacyon                               x^ll x^s
                Summa xl^ll etc.
        It' of Swyne Grett and small xv pis             xxv
        It' of pecoks pehens and other birds
          in all viiij p's                           x^s  ⎫
        It' of Ducks Draks, yong and olde                 ⎬ per
          xxiiij p's                                  v^s ⎬ est.
        It' of Poolen etc. abowt the howse                ⎮
          xxiiij p's                                  v^s ⎭
        The Stedd.
        The lytell chamber where I do lye.
my wyf. ex'  Itm a joyned bedsted of oke wyth a
             trokell bed  under it, bought of mr
             poole at                                   iiij^s
my wyf. ex'  Itm a tester to the same with iij curtens
             all of read and grene saye  p'ice          vj^s
my w. ex'    It' a new corse Mattres uppon the
             same pis                                    ij^s
my w.        It' ij fether bedds with one bolster
             lying on the same bedsted, eyther of
             them beyng j yerde iij q^ts brode p'ce
             for both                                 liij^s iiij^d
my w. ex'    It' a lytell tabyll bord  p'ce             xx^d
             It' a playne lytell turky carpet  p'ce   xj^s viij^d
my w. ex'    It' ij Cusshons of red fflanel wrought
             with cruell and stuffyd with ffethers
             p'ce of both                             iiij^s iiij^d
my w. ex'    It' a pece of olde tapestry hengyng and
             lyned with canvas, all conteynyng in
             depth about iij yards and in length
             iij yards di'  p'ce                         v^s
my w. ex'    It' a olde pece of red and grene heng-
             gyng over the Chymely etc. worth at       viij^d
my w. ex'    It' ij woollen blanketts p'is          ij^s viij^d
my w. ex'    It' a small coverlet of tapestre  p'ce   viij^s
my w.        It' ij pylowes of downe covered with
             fustyan                                   iiij^s
E. M.        It' a superaltare in a lynen bag at      iiij^d
                                                   4.  17  4.
```

GLOSSARY

Alman Ryvetts: 'Light armour so called because they be buckled or rivetted after the old Alman (German) fashion.'

Alter Cloth: the upper altar cloth would now be called the dossal; the 'nether' being in modern nomenclature the altar-frontal.

Alterpylo: a pillow or cushion on which to lay the mass book.

Alter Tablett: a triptych with folding doors, containing three carved images;

the Blessed Virgin Mary and (probably) two attendant saints.

Awmbry: dresser or chest.

Bankes: 'bankes' formerly signified a cloth or carpet or tapestry for forms or benches (*bancs*) hence any kind of small coverlet.

Bawdekyn: silk brocade, so called from its manufacture at Baghdad (Italian Baldacca).

Beame: with six latten candlesticks: probably intended for festal use in the chapel.

Bods of Alman Ryvetts (QV): 6 bods here seem to mean 6 'sets' of light armour, in which case it must be connected with the obscure and obsolete past participle 'boden', provided with arms, accoutred.

Carpet: a covering for a table, not a floor.

Celor: the canopy of a bed.

Cloyster: where this was situated we have no means of judging; it may only have been a penthouse. There was nothing monastic about the old house at Markeaton.

Cobyerons: 'cob irons', andirons; the dogs of a fireplace – the irons on which the spit, etc. is supported.

Counterborde: a sideboard or cupboard.

Crepars of yeron: 'creepers', small low irons in a grate to keep the fire from spreading.

Crucifix, Picture of the: the description would suit very well the detached hood of a cope, on which was often represented the Crucifixion with attendant figures.

Cruell: 'crewel', thin worsted yarn for tapestry and embroidery.

Curtall: a horse with a docked tail.

Drege: 'drege', a mixture of different kinds of grain grown together.

Fustyan: 'fustian', originally a fabric of some distinction made at Fustat but here employed in its modern sense of strong cotton cloth.

Garnish of vesel: a service of pewter plate.

Goorgets: 'gorget' a defence for the neck.

Images of apostles, etc: orphreys for a cope or some such vestment.

Jacks: Leather coats.

King's Majesty's Book: King Henry VIII's Primer, published 1545.

Kynell: a form of 'kimnell'; a tub used for various purposes. In the brewhouse; 'Knedying tubs or kynnells'.

Latten: a fine quality of brass used for sepulchral monuments, crosses, etc.

Lomys: 'loom', 'lome', 'lume', any kind of vessel.

Maase of steele: a steel mace, fighting weapon.

Mene potts: middle sized pots.

Panyd: a curtain etc. was 'paned' when formed of long narrow stripes or 'panes' of different patterns or colours sewn together. The letters J&M are probably the initials of Sir John Mundy.

Paynted tables: pictures on panel, Sir John Mundy's arms were granted to him in 1510.

Portes: a breviary.

Possenet: A 'posnet' or little pot.

Pottel pots of pewter: 'pottle' a liquid measure of four pints; 'pottle pot', a two-quart pot or tankard.

Pynnys of silver: silver pins.

St John's Cloth: either a covering for an image of St John or (more probably) a case for a 'St John's tablet' of alabaster, of which a good many examples are known.

Saletts: were head pieces.

Saye: 'serge' the tester of a bed was the fixed top and head parts.

Scormer: 'scummer', a shallow ladle or sieve for removing scum or floating matter from the surface of a liquid.

Splents: 'splints', armour for arms.

Steyned canvas: with representations of the Trinity and the visit of the Magi.

Tables: 'a payr of tables' was what we should call a backgammon board.

Trevett: a trivet.

Trokell bed: 'truckle-bed', on castors which was kept under the large bed and pulled out when required.

Trundelbed: 'trundle-bed', a small bed on wheels or castors.

Trussing bed; a travelling bed, made to pack.

Turned Chayre: a chair of which the frame was turned on a lathe.

Twynts: two-year old cattle (two winters).

Vambrace: armour covering the forearm from wrist to elbow.

Verders: a kind of tapestry.

Vestement: here the term, which strictly indicates a chasuble, is extended as is often the case, to include the complete set necessary for the celebration of Mass. Here the alb is noted as lacking.

In 1755 Wrightson Mundy pulled down the old hall and replaced it with what has rightly been described as a 'dignified brick edifice'. He may have been motivated by the fact that 10 years earlier German Pole of neighbouring Radbourne had had a very fine new hall

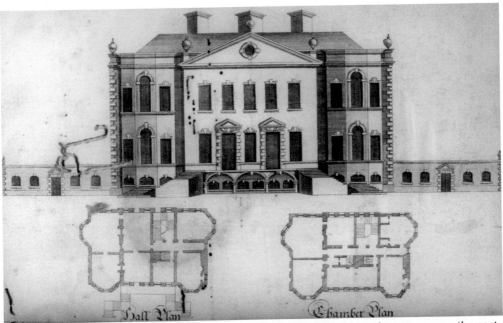

Engraving from an architect's drawing for the new hall, 1755. This shows the entrance on the east front but the actual building had the entrance facing west. The drawing is badly worm eaten.
(Derby Museum and Art Gallery)

The east front of the new Markeaton Hall *c.*1790–1810. Compare this with the architect's drawing. *(Private collection)*

The east front of Markeaton Hall seen in 1858. An extension has been added to the north and a portico shelters the new main entrance. The portico was removed in 1904 and replaced by twin-domed conservatories. *(Derby Local Studies Library)*

designed and built by the fashionable architect, William Smith of Warwick. The new one at Markeaton was designed, in collaboration with Wrightson Mundy, by the less well known James Denstone of Derby (1724–1780), but they nonetheless succeeded in producing a very pleasant building. The interior contained much classical decoration in the form of wrought iron and stucco work, the ceiling of the music room being especially notable. Wrightson's

A rather faded view of the west front in 1858. This is a typical photograph of the period with carefully posed figures. *(Derby Local Studies Library)*

son, Francis Noel Clark Mundy, commissioned Joseph Pickford, a highly esteemed local architect, to build an orangery and stable block around a double courtyard to replace the remaining Tudor outbuildings and these, as already mentioned, still stand, partly built on the existing stone foundations.

Incorporated into this block were the kitchens, which were fitted with what were then the very latest in cooking ranges and a boiler to provide constant hot water. The kitchens were connected to the hall by an underground passage and survived till the 1980s when they, in turn, were demolished, although one of the original ranges was rescued and is preserved by Derby Museum. Sometime around the turn of the 18th to 19th century an extension was added to the north and the main entrance was moved from the west front to the east. The portico to this entrance was removed in 1904 and rebuilt in the grounds as a summer house. It still exists in a dilapidated condition in the west corner of the gardens by the tennis courts. It was replaced by fashionable, twin-domed conservatories, built by Messenger of Loughborough, which later became known by the none too dignified title of the 'Markeaton Mae Wests'!

Eighteenth-century cooking range from the kitchen, which was demolished in the early 1980s. It was preserved by Derby Museum.

57

Two views of the east front of the hall in 1964, shortly before its demolition. One shows the twin conservatories and the other the mulberry tree, which fortunately still flourishes. *(Derby Evening Telegraph)*

The west front shortly before demolition. *(Derby City Council Leisure Services)*

Within the hall someone must have had a full time job cleaning out the firegrates, as there were no fewer than 60 chimneys in various groups on the roof, although some of them may have been blanks for appearance only. Equally, somebody must have been fully occupied providing fuel, even if the fireplaces were not all in use at the same time. Although coal was certainly used, a lot of wood was burned as well and it was no coincidence that the woodyard was quite close by on the west drive. Coal was also used by the estate tenants, as one entry in Mrs Emily Mundy's account book shows the weekly income of the workers to

have been three shillings a day for a six-day week plus six pence worth of coal. There was one fireplace surround of carved oak that is considered, from an existing photograph, to be so old that it almost certainly came from the previous hall. There were also three

Joseph Pickford's Orangery was later added to the hall and is now the only remaining part of it. It is currently in use as a café. *(Derby Evening Telegraph)*

Aerial view from the west taken in 1958. A rare view of the roof with its 60 chimneys and the bell housing. The circular fountain can be seen between the steps. The centre block in the stable yard has since been demolished and the area now houses a craft village. *(H. Tempest Ltd, Cardiff)*

Adam fireplaces. On the roof was a bell which was rung to tell the estate workers when to start and when to finish work.

Of the contents and furnishings of the hall we fortunately have some knowledge, as much of it was listed in the Sale Catalogue of April 1930. The catalogue was far too extensive to reproduce here in its entirety, but extracts from it give a good idea of the type and quality of the contents and show a marked contrast in both quantity and quality to what was owned by Vincent Mundy in 1545, as seen earlier in this section.

Only the furnishings of the library were listed as the books were sold separately. From the dining room, item 422, a six pedestal dining table, realised the then considerable sum of two hundred guineas and the vendor, the Revd Prebendary William Gilchrist Clark-

A series of excellent *Derby Evening Telegraph* photographs fortuitously taken a few months prior to demolition. Without this we would have no record of the interior of this lovely hall: Bay window, east front; Carved wooden door; Fireplace in the Music Room on the first floor; Ceiling in the Music Room; Recess with serving table to the Dining Room. First floor; Main staircase from the ground floor; Staircase; Entrance Hall. Fireplace surround which is much older than the building; probably came from the previous hall; Two views on the roof showing the balustrade and the bell.

Maxwell, heir to Mrs Mundy's estate, used this to finance a cruise to the Holy Land for himself, his wife and younger son. On the ship was a widow with two eligible daughters, to the elder of whom the Clark-Maxwell son, John Noel, was very much attracted. This resulted in marriage and in due course the birth of the present holder of Markeaton, Charles Clark-Maxwell.

Listed among the outdoor sundries was a punt, which seems not to have been sold as the author remembers one decaying for many years by the boathouse into the late 1940s when the lake was dredged and made suitable again for public boating. Also among the sundries was a Sedan basket chair, which was used by Mrs Mundy in her latter years. Mrs Mundy commissioned a photograph to be taken of herself in this chair, wrapped in her shawl and bonnet. A now unknown number of copies were made and distributed and on each one everything was painted over in watercolour except for the face and one hand, which remained as photographic images. The pictures are unsigned but there is a distinct possibility that the lady herself painted them. Quite what the purpose of these unusual portraits was is not known, but certainly each one was unique apart from the face and hand.

SECOND DAY'S SALE.

Thursday, April 10th, 1930.

AT 11 A.M.

NOTE—All Lots marked with an asterisk will be left in house and sold from, and in order of Catalogue.

BEDROOM No. 10.

334 Steel fender and firesteels and hearthrug
335 Japanned coal vase and hip bath
336 Bronze figured Brussels carpet, 7×6 yards approx.
337 Mahogany set of bedsteps
338 Walnut couch, upholstered
339 Rosewood fold-top card table, on pedestal, 3'
340 Walnut oval occasional table, banded tulip wood
341 Mahogany armchair covered in striped green tapestry
342 *4' 6" brass-mounted bedstead, with hair mattress, feather bolster and pillow
343 Pair of brass candlesticks and pair of oak stands
344 Quantity of toilet ware

BEDROOM No. 11.

345 Copper helmet coal bucket
346 Walnut settee, upholstered, and with loose cretonne cover
347 Armchair covered in crimson rep
348 Antique oblong mahogany pedestal table, 4' 8"×3' 6"
349 Walnut writing table with two drawers and inlaid leather top
350 Mahogany circular pedestal cupboard
351 Walnut towel airer
352 Carrying chair
353 *Skeleton wardrobe and chintz curtain

LOT
491 PAIR OF 24" CHINESE IMARI BALUSTER-SHAPED VASES AND COVERS, with alternate panels of birds in landscape and oriental flowers, surmounted with wood gilt finials (cover damaged)
492 33" Chinese Imari vase, similar, with octagonal-shaped dome cover, decorated with flowering trees
493 32" CHINESE BLUE AND WHITE VASE, baluster-shaped body, decorated with figures, with Kylin surmount (damaged), Kang-shi period
494 Pair of 8½" Derby candlesticks, the columns and bases decorated scrollwork, painted flowers and fruit, blue and gilt borders
495 Pair of 8½" china vases, with tapering sides, alternate panels, salmon and white, gilt ring handles and borders
496 Pair of old Chinese glazed white china doves, 6½", on metal bases, with olive branches (one damaged)
497 Derby sucrier and cover, with fluted body, white with gilt bands, three cups, saucer and coffee can, similar
498 Six Salopian cups, two saucers, and slop basin, white, with sprays of flowers, blue and gold and interior bands
499 9½" Chinese familie verte vase and cover (damaged), two Chinese blue and white 8½" plates, and 8" shallow bowl, similar
500 Seven Derby coffee cans and four large teacups (damaged)
501 10" DERBY VASE AND COVER, deep blue ground, encrusted with flowers, decorated gilt butterflies
502 A similar lot
503 Pair of blue and white Chinese teapots, surmounted with Kylins, and pair of coffee pots to match
504 Small Chinese blue and white teapot, coffee pot, Japanese teapot, blue and white mug, and candlestick
505 Two Staffordshire jugs, cup, and two saucers, white, with blue and yellow bands
506 Bloor Derby pen-and-ink stand, deep crimson, with gilt borders, on oblong stand, having inkpot, pounce box and cover, and taper stick
507 Pair of 13" oriental vases and covers, rectangular bodies, with long tapering necks, having mauve panels, decorated flowers

GROUND FLOOR.

OLD KITCHEN & BASEMENT PASSAGE.

LOT
136-145 Sundry furniture
146 Set of five steps, wood rack and sundries
147 Large meat safe
148 Mahogany pedestal, mahogany towel airer, three satinwood pole fire-screens and banners and ebonized chair
149 Iron folding bed, iron bedstead, fire steels, slop pail, and cast-iron umbrella stand
150 Two engravings in gilt, two small oil paintings
151 Croquet set
152 Patent oil stove and two wicker baskets
153 Wood metal-lined hot plate
154 Smoker's birch armchair and a similar chair with cane seat and back

OLD SERVANTS' HALL.

155 Three mahogany-framed chairs, old fowling piece, etc.
156 Antique mahogany towel airer
157 " Perfection " oil stove, Bissel's carper sweeper and two cane chairs
158 Roll of cocoa matting
159 " Acme " wringer
160 *STUART PERIOD CARVED OAK SIDE TABLE, with six baluster legs and carved frieze, in conventional leaf design, 9' 8" long, 2' 9" wide

BUTLER'S PANTRY.

161 Deal kitchen table with three drawers and two lath-back chairs
162 Six various waiters, mahogany knife box
163 Six hot water cans
164 Eight smaller ditto

LOT
244 *ANTIQUE MAHOGANY SLOPE-TOP WRITING DESK with small drawers above, centre drawer, on hoof feet
245 PAIR OF CHIPPENDALE MAHOGANY CHAIRS with split ladder backs and dip seats

LIBRARY.

246 Antique pierced-front steel fender, two cut steels and stands
247 *Plate-glass mantel mirror in gilt wood frame, with three pillars at each side and ball frieze, 3' 6"×4' 1"
248 Japanned coal vase on wheels
249 Maple shaped-top table, foot rest and two footstools
250 Lounge chair upholstered in crimson rep, and feather cushion
251 Winged easy chair covered in figured cretonne, and flock cushion
252 *Rosewood circular pedestal dining table, 4' 6" diameter
253 Mahogany two-tier dinner waggon on castors, 4' wide
254 Antique mahogany side-table on four supports, with carved cross-stretchers, 3' 3" wide
255 Invalid's chair with cane seat and back
256 Set of mahogany folding steps
257 Four plaster busts
258 Pair of plaster ornaments, Man and Woman seated on pedestals, holding pitchers, and a 17" figure of Venus de Milo
259 Pair of potteryware dishes in forms of hens seated on nests
260 Carved white marble figure of Dutch Girl, 13"

TOP STAIRCASE & LANDING.

261 Thirty heavy circular brass stair rods
262 Pair of long crimson silk damask curtains
263 *Painted store cupboard with shelves above, and three drawers below, 10' high, 2' 6" wide
264 *White enamelled winged wardrobe, centre partition fitted with shelves, and drawer below, 8' 10" wide, 7' high
265 Pine commode and circular folding table
266 " Perfection " oil stove, iron stand, four-tier stand, and painted pole firescreen

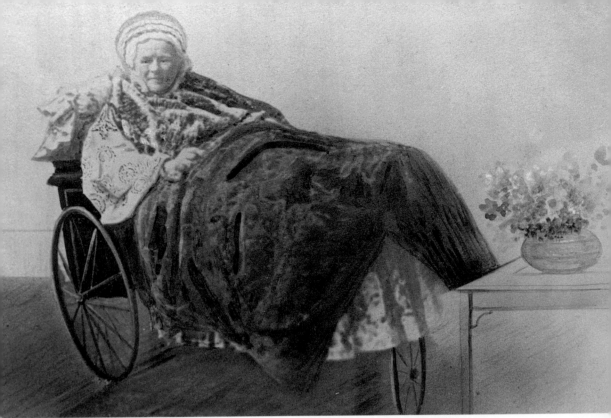

The remarkable portrait of Mrs Emily Mundy in her sedan basket chair. It is painted over a photograph, leaving only the face and hand untouched, and may even have been painted by the lady herself. *(Private collection)*

The author is aware of two existing copies and is interested to know (via the publisher) of any others.

As one modern feature not to be found in the hall was a bathroom, some of the bedrooms contained hip baths and, right to the end of her life, Mrs Mundy bathed by the fire in her private apartment. And what could be pleasanter! Also notable in some of the bedrooms were mahogany commodes. The all too obvious plumbing on the east front of the building (see p58) was added after her death.

About the same time that Pickford was working on the Orangery the adjacent park was landscaped in the then fashionable manner adopted by the nationally famous Lancelot 'Capability' Brown. Markeaton Park extends to about 180 acres and was laid out by William Emes, a local man of considerable talents (see *Varieties*). There were formal gardens, shaded walks and a lake which was created by widening the Markeaton Brook.

Not all of Emes's work has survived but some of the longer-lived trees, such as oaks and yews, remain to remind us of his artistry.

Dining table from the hall, item No. 422 in the sale catalogue of April 1930. Sold for 200 guineas. See text. *(Private collection)*

The end of an era in November 1964. *(Author)*

In spite of the impression of secluded tranquility, life at the hall was not always so peaceful. In 1831 the Bill for the Reform of Parliament was passed by the Commons but thrown out by the Lords. The working classes rioted, wrecking local business premises and attacking private houses. The gaol was broken open and the prisoners released. Anyone who had been against the Bill was fair game for the mob and this included the Mundys, whose hall was surrounded and the windows broken before the menservants could beat them off. Even then the situation was so tense that Mrs Harriot Mundy did not undress for four nights. Eventually the Mayor read the Riot Act in the Market Place and order was restored by the Yeomanry.

On her death in 1929 Mrs Emily Mundy bequeathed the hall and gardens to the Derby Borough Council, to be used 'for the purposes of an Art Gallery or Museum or other municipal purpose of a similar character or as a recreation centre for the inhabitants of Derby'. The most that came from this was the opening of a café which advertised the then fashionable 'Teas With Hovis'. There was also a suggestion that the hall could be used as a convalescent facility for the Derbyshire Royal Infirmary. Apart from the café Mrs Mundy's request obviously fell on deaf ears as the said council then allowed the hall to deteriorate until World War Two, when it was commandeered for six years by the military, who left it in a state of considerable disrepair, even robbing it of some of its finer features such as fireplaces. After the war it languished, still blatantly neglected by a council who plainly had no intention of carrying out Mrs Mundy's wishes, until 1964, by which time its condition was such that demolition was the only remedy.

Thus its fate was sealed and the remaining internal fittings were removed and presumably acquired by dealers. Even in that final crucial council meeting the opinion was expressed that it represented the 'oppressive capital-owning classes and was better destroyed' and one is led to the conclusion that its condition was not the only factor that

The classical fountain brought from Venice c.1798. This 'disappeared' during the demolition of 1964 and 'reappeared' about 30 years later. It currently stands in Derwent Park. (Author)

This charming 1935 photograph shows, top centre, one of the pair of cast-iron urns by Andrew Handyside which have long since 'gone missing'. In the foreground is Miss Gwen Smedley with her nephew David Ordish, both well in fashion for dress and child transport. (Private collection)

led to its demise. The bell was reputedly bought by a Scout group, but its present whereabouts are unknown to the author. The orangery survives as a pleasant café while the other outbuildings have been converted into that modern phenomenon now considered essential by many well-known estates, a craft village.

The site of the hall is covered by an extension to the gardens which contains a circular feature that purports to be a fountain but which for a long while has served little purpose beyond that of collecting rubbish. If it is intended to replace the classical marble fountain, which was brought from Venice by Francis Mundy in around 1798 and which stood within the curve of the hall steps, then it has fallen a long way short of the mark both aesthetically and practically. Along with other valuable items this fountain vanished when the hall was destroyed and its whereabouts were unknown for many years until it reputedly miraculously reappeared in a roadside ditch in Leicestershire. It was transported to Derby and may now be seen restored and re-erected in Derwent Park. The new wall at the east end of the gardens houses the wrought-iron gates which formerly stood by the main entrance on Ashbourne Road.

When the park was acquired by the council a lot of effort was put into making it more than just a place to walk or picnic, although plenty of space was left for those particular pastimes. An 18-hole pitch and putt course, a putting green and tennis courts were laid out and boating introduced on the lake, which was considerably enlarged from the one William Emes had created. As well as rowing boats, rides in a motor boat were also popular. In a field a little to the north of the hall a children's paddling pool was installed. Unfortunately, with the onset of World War Two, the whole of the park to the south of the lake was commandeered by the army and turned into a large camp. There were rows of wooden barrack blocks, parade grounds and other main buildings made of brick and when hostilities ceased some of these were used as temporary housing for people left homeless by six years of destruction and no new building. Of those buildings only two now survive and one of them serves as an engine shed for one of the park's popular attractions, the recently laid narrow gauge steam railway. This runs round much of the park boundary from the main drive to the Mundy Play Centre, which has superseded the simple paddling pool. Here there are numerous activities for children including a new pool (originally with a fountain but this was removed in 2001 for safety reasons), as the old one is no longer suitable and is now frequented only by water birds, canoes and radio-controlled model boats. The park, fortunately, fared better than the hall and is fairly well kept and attractive despite the recent national financial restraints and the advent of the A38 extension.

1921 view of the lodge at the main gate on Ashbourne Road. It was demolished in 1935. *(Derby Museum and Art Gallery)*

Early 1930s view of the enlarged lake and the newly planted islands. *(Hurst and Wallis)*

Another 1930s view of the enlarged lake and the newly planted islands. *(Hurst and Wallis)*

The new bridge near the head of the lake, seen during construction in the early 1930s.

The portico removed from the hall in 1904. It now stands in dilapidated condition at the western extremity of the gardens. *(Author)*

The completed new bridge from the east.

Looking across the formal terrace gardens to the Orangery with a former estate cottage at the left. *(Derby Evening Telegraph)*

A 1905 photograph of the terrace and Orangery with Mrs Emily Mundy on the steps.

Groups of trees planted by William Emes interspersed with older specimens.
(Author)

'The Poachers Tree', an old oak once used by poachers from the West End who sheltered in it for a quick cigarette without being seen. At least 500 years old, it was regrettably burned out early in 2003.
(Author)

William Emes made extensive use of yew trees in the park. This row is by the wall of the stable yard. *(Author)*

The old mulberry tree which until recently stood near the hall site. *(Author)*

Possibly a 1930s view of the paddling pool, one of the early attractions to be installed in the park after it was acquired by the council. The hillside behind was part of the Markeaton Golf Course, which was built on soon after the end of World War Two. *(W.W. Winter)*

A 1960s view of a waterless paddling pool when it was drained for health reasons. The area has since been superseded by the modern Mundy Play Centre. In the background is the new Technical College, later, in much extended form, to become Derby University. *(Author)*

The Pitch and Putt course laid out across the fossilised remains of mediaeval ridge and furrow fields. *(Author)*

All good parks had a bandstand and Markeaton was no exception. This photograph was taken in snow in the early 1950s. The bandstand has since been removed. *(Author)*

The Pets' Cemetery with a 19th-century memorial to Tina, a fox terrier, and an unmarked mediaeval column possibly marking the grave of a horse. The origins of the column are unknown. *(Author)*

An old thatched cottage which stood on the west drive, sometimes known as the Ghost House. This survived the mid-18th-century village clearance but not the 1960s one. *(Private collection)*

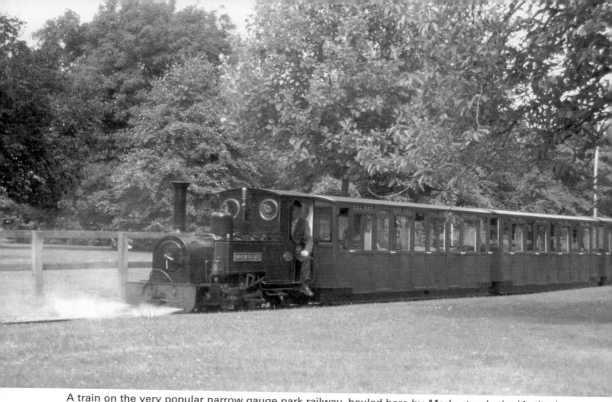

A train on the very popular narrow gauge park railway, hauled here by *Markeaton Lady. (Author)*

Early 20th-century scene in the wood yard. *(Private collection)*

The former bridge to the park from Kedleston Road near the Markeaton Golf Club house. The university now occupies the background. *(Private collection)*

Markeaton Park main entrance, December 1940. The roof is that of the guardhouse which, during civil occupation after the war, became a Co-op store. *(Derby Evening Telegraph)*

The park during military occupation in World War Two. *(Derby Evening Telegraph)*

The brick building was the army cookhouse with outdoor ovens. It is currently used as the engine shed for the light railway. *(Derby Evening Telegraph)*

CHAPTER SIX

The Roads . . .

Roman

Soon after their arrival in the Derby area the Romans built a road almost due west to link up with their fort at Rocester. The standard Roman road was built on a bank or agger, to give it its technical name, with ditches on either side, thus affording some height advantage in case of assault. This one was probably surfaced with rammed gravel, of which there is an abundance in the district. Reminders of this fact are contained in the names Markeaton Stones and Gravel Pit Wood. The exact line of the road, from Little Chester to a point west of Brun Lane by the former Wheathills Farm, is mainly lost, but by looking at some of the evidence still available to us we can be reasonably sure that it was a typically straight road. From that point in the fields near Wheathills Farm the alignment can be clearly seen from the air and, for much of the way to Rocester, it can also be traced on the ground. Roman roads were frequently used as territorial boundaries by those coming later and even today many miles of vanished road can be followed on maps and across the countryside by using hedges or walls as a guide.

So it is at Markeaton and Mackworth. We can trace its course through the manor from what was formerly the corner of Broadway and Kedleston Road before the A38 was opened in 1983. Somewhere near here, between Broadway and Maxwell Avenue, the Roman road passed on its way across the park to the head of the lake by the boathouse. This is confirmed by a hedgerow which appears on the enclosure map. From there it followed the line of the present park drive, out through the west gate and along the short section of Markeaton Lane to where this makes a sharp left turn south to Ashbourne Road. A stream passes under the road at this point and in 1938 the stream was culverted. During this operation a section of road 'of Roman type' was observed by a reliable local historian in the trench cut across the lane. It was not archaeologically investigated but is nonetheless a possible confirmation of the line of the road. Twenty-five years later, in 1963, workmen laying drainage to a house in Markeaton hamlet found the old surface again, but unfortunately this was not reported and again no record was made.

The line of the Roman road through Markeaton. The Roman surface was found by the house on the left in 1963 and also at a point behind the camera in 1938. The house on the right has been demolished and is now a nursery garden. In the centre is the village green. *(Private collection)*

From the bend in the lane the road can be followed quite closely, but not exactly, by a footpath through the fields to Mackworth Church. This section can also be traced on the map by the line of hedgerows. This footpath was surfaced with gravel till it was ploughed out to the absolute legal minimum in the 1980s, since when its surface has largely disappeared under soil. The gravel surface is, of course, not Roman, as it has been in use for many hundreds of years since and has therefore been remetalled. The road then passed through what is now Mackworth churchyard to the south of the church and continued straight on until it crossed the present Lower Road very near to the so-called Castle gateway. Having climbed the bank on a still traceable terrace it crossed the A52 Ashbourne Road, emerging from the field at the corner of Jarvey's Lane and cutting across behind the house on the corner of Brun Lane. Again the map shows a hedge on line.

Beside this road, some time after the Roman retreat, were founded two villages and for many years it must have been the main communication link between them. It does not appear on the *c*.1755 map but this is probably due to the fact that it was only fenced on one side and conventional signs for unfenced roads did not exist then. In any case, it is very unlikely that it ever went out of use. By 1836 the OS map shows it quite clearly and the late Mrs Emily Mundy, who died in 1929, used it regularly on her way to church, for which

Hollow way of the old entrance to Markeaton Hall, later known as the 'Side Gate', looking towards the hall site. *(Author)*

occasions it was always carefully raked and levelled on the Saturday, hence its former well metalled condition.

Mediaeval

In the early days of Markeaton a track would have joined it to its nearest neighbour to the east, Northworthy or, as the Vikings renamed it, Deoraby. The line of this ancient way is still marked by Markeaton Street (formerly Markeaton Lane) and its line passed close by the hall on the present West Drive. This way has had a chequered life as it went out of use before 1755, possibly to keep travellers away from the hall, and a new entrance to the park was made from the mediaeval road to Ashbourne. This can be seen on the *c.*1755 map and is still very distinct on the ground as a deep hollow way at the top of the hill on the south side of the park, from where it led directly to the gateway in the old hall complex (see *Markeaton Hall*).

However, a map of Derby from Lewis's *Topographical Dictionary* of 1831 shows very clearly a continuation of Markeaton Street running straight to the hall, while the one on the hill to the south is marked simply as the Side Gate. This situation is confirmed by the OS one-inch map of 1836, but by 1852 the direct route had again vanished from the map and terminated, a little way short of where Queensway now passes, at a house which is still there

Line of the mediaeval Ashbourne Road looking towards Derby. Along this road some of Bonnie Prince Charlie's army marched on Derby in December 1745. Behind the bushes, to the left of centre in the photograph, the junction of the north loop to lower Mackworth still exists, although it is badly overgrown. *(Author)*

called North Lodge. If this was a lodge of Markeaton Hall then its name is peculiar as it lies south-east of the hall and we are at a loss to know what it was north of.

The line of the mediaeval road from Derby to the far side of Mackworth, as shown on the map, can still be traced with the exception of one or two short lengths. Starting with the present junction of Ashbourne Road with the A38/Derby ring road, the line of the mediaeval one is at first under the A52 but near the top of the hill it turned slightly north and can be followed through the line of trees on the south edge of the park. A little way to the west of the park it divided to form a loop which rejoined to become a single road again at Bow Bridge near the site of the Indian restaurant.

The south fork continued straight on past the edge of the municipal crematorium grounds until it crossed Markeaton Lane. The line of the road is visible to the east of Markeaton Lane as a hollow way marked by a recent line of trees and as a hedgerow to the west of the lane. From this point it turned south to the junction with Radbourne Lane and thereafter it followed roughly the line of the A52 until it met the other half of the loop at Bow Bridge. Just before reaching Brun Lane it curved south round where a house now stands high up on the corner and on the far side of the lane a small remaining section of hollow way can still be seen in the field.

A green lane by the gate to Mackworth Church, as seen in 1983, where it joins Lower Road, having crossed Markeaton Lane after diverging from the main road near the park. This is part of the mediaeval road system. *(Author)*

From the park the other fork turned north-west across what is now the crematorium field, crossed Markeaton Lane and went down the slope opposite until it emerged by the gate to Mackworth Church, where a short section of it can still be seen as a green lane. The road across the crematorium field was gone by 1767, according to Burdett. Perhaps the turnpiking of the Ashbourne Road had rendered this section redundant and, as the field was probably still in use for agricultural purposes, the old road would have been ploughed out. It is certainly untraceable today.

From the gateway to Mackworth Church the mediaeval way followed the line of the present Lower Road (formerly Town Street) through the village until it reached the bottom of Jarvey's Lane. Here, where the lane turns south up the hill, the old road went straight on before curving down to Bow Bridge to meet the other half of the loop. At one time this section could be clearly seen in the fields. The short, straight stretch from Lower Road is still visible in the grass but the part that curved down to Bow Bridge, complete with kerbstones, ditches and some paving, was filled in during the autumn of 1982 and is now only marked by a line of trees across the field. Fortunately this feature is recorded on two aerial photographs, but to date no ground view has been located.

This mediaeval road is the very one along which part of Bonnie Prince Charlie's army marched in December 1745. They were not deployed in one neat column, but were spread wide across the countryside so that some of them came from Kedleston via Markeaton Stones while others came by Long Lane. This approach ensured that they would get all they could from villages and farms along the way, by whatever means were necessary, for these soldiers had marched a very long way and were hungry. As Wrightson Mundy and German Pole of Radbourne were staunch Jacobite sympathisers they probably did fairly well locally, as the estate tenants would hardly dare to refuse. Also, at that stage, they still believed that they faced the long march to London.

At Mackworth the two parallel sides of the loop were joined by four lanes: Jarvey's Lane, Gold Lane, one now lost and another, which is now a stream, has been replaced on a new alignment by Church Lane. This latter is proved by an aerial photograph which shows the ridge and furrow cut by the later lane. In the village there were also back lanes leading to crofts and some can be traced as slight hollow ways. Part of the continuation of Gold Lane to the north of Lower Road is still a deep cutting, overgrown and muddy and hidden between two farms. These were recorded on maps as late as 1860 and two still exist as farm tracks on the north side of the brook.

Other mediaeval roads in the area, still in use, are Markeaton Lane, the old road to Kedleston (now a farm track past Markeaton Stones) and another former track which has since been developed to form the present Kedleston Road. Brun Lane, Radbourne Lane and Windmill Hill Lane are all shown on the map.

Finally, the map also shows a track running north to south from the elbow in Markeaton Lane to Ashbourne Road. This was gone by 1831 and presumably suffered the same fate as the one across the crematorium field, vanishing under the plough.

Turnpike onward

The act authorising the turnpiking of the Derby to Ashbourne road was passed in 1738. Until then the roads were in a terrible condition, all but impassable in bad weather and often unsuitable for vehicles. Certainly the well-preserved but now buried length near the Indian restaurant was far too narrow for anything but horses or, at most, a very small cart. Turnpiking involved the setting up for each road of a Turnpike Trust, usually a group of locally influential men, which would organise and supervise the improvements to be carried out. The first task of these trustees was to produce an income from the road in their care and this was done by erecting toll-gates and houses on existing roads. As money became available so work was carried out, but frequently this was to those sections of most interest and personal advantage to the trustees! Gradually, over many years, sections of road were straightened and rerouted and gradients eased. Burdett's map of 1767 shows some definite changes in the Markeaton and Mackworth area and by 1836 the OS one-inch map shows the main A52 Ashbourne Road on virtually the alignment we know today.

On the corner of the slightly extended Markeaton Lane was a toll-house, and this was still standing in the early 1920s until it was reputedly demolished by an out-of-control Trent bus or lorry, but versions of the story vary. This particular toll-gate apparently controlled the passage of vehicles and livestock using Markeaton Lane. Another toll-house was sited in an old cottage on Kedleston Road, opposite the end of Maxwell Avenue (demolished in 1928), but it was replaced nearer to the end of Markeaton Lane by a purpose-built one which still stands, minus its characteristic bay window, which was removed in the 1960s by,

Two views of the Toll House on the corner of Ashbourne Road and Markeaton Lane. It was reputedly demolished by a Trent bus in around 1922. *(Derby Museum and Art Gallery)*

Mediaeval road to the west of Mackworth. It can be seen in the grass, just beyond the farm in the foreground. The section that curves to the left has since been buried and can only be traced by a line of trees. *(Copyright reserved Cambridge University Collection of Air Photographs)*

Toll House on the corner of Windmill Hill Lane and Ashbourne Road. *(Derby Museum and Art Gallery)*

Kedleston Road *c.*1928, looking from where the A38 now crosses. The cottages on the left served as the first Toll House here but were superseded in the 19th century by a purpose-built one, which is visible in the distance at the centre of the picture. At the right of this view is the clubhouse of the Markeaton Golf Club.

guess what, an out-of-control lorry. Perhaps someone who was forced to pay for what had always been free travel put a curse on them! A third gate and house were sited on Ashbourne Road at the corner of Windmill Hill Lane and the house was for a while concerned with communication, being used as a mobile phone shop.

The very straightness of the new Ashbourne Road misled the late Ivan Margary, in his excellent book *The Roman Roads of Britain*, into suggesting that this might have been built on the Roman alignment, but subsequent research has shown this to be incorrect. Margary, in covering the whole of Britain, could not possibly have gone into local detail and there is no implied criticism here of his suggesting an alternative to the then untraced section of the road from Little Chester.

About 1927 work commenced on the new Derby Arterial Road and three sections of this, Kingsway, Queensway and Broadway, cut through the estate. Today Kingsway and Queensway, in much widened form, are part of the A38 trunk road and our peaceful park is bounded on one side by the busiest and noisiest road in the area. Finally, in 1936 a new road was proposed as part of the flood relief scheme (see *...and the Water*), which would

The 'new' Toll House on
Kedleston Road, 1895. The
bay window was demolished
by a lorry in the 1960s.
*(Derby Museum and Art
Gallery)*

In this view of Ashbourne Road the park entrance is on the left. The whole of the visible wall was removed to make way for Queensway and the Markeaton island. The photograph was taken from near where a filling station now stands. (*Derby Local Studies Library*)

have taken the bends out of Markeaton Lane, but this part of the scheme was not completed, an embankment in the field behind the Old Forge being the only reminder of the idea. The building of good roads put many of the old ones into disuse. We are indeed fortunate in this area in having so many of them still traceable and in such variety, Roman, mediaeval and modern, each with its own history intertwined with the others and each one, at some point, crossing the others.

Roadside boundary post now in Derby Industrial Museum. (*Author*)

CHAPTER SEVEN

. . . and the Water

WHEN the sites of Markeaton and Mackworth were first selected, one of the prime considerations was the availability of water. As well as springs for domestic water, Markeaton was abundantly supplied as it was close to the confluence of two brooks, which have long borne the names of the two villages. From this point the resulting single stream proceeded to the east, where it eventually joined the River Derwent close to the present

Early 20th-century view of Markeaton Brook as it enters the park near Markeaton Lane. The field behind the fence is now the Mundy Play Centre. *(Private collection)*

The same scene today. *(Author)*

A photograph by F.W. Scarratt from *c.*1912.

A 19th-century engraving of Markeaton Brook.

The mill leat behind the nursery gardens. This feeds the ornamental waterfall at the head of the lake. *(Author)*

The newly landscaped Domesday mill site as it appeared in 1935. The Dower house on the left was demolished in the 1960s. *(Douglas A. Farnsworth)*

Council House and River Gardens. Although now diverted to a point lower down the river, the disused entrance point into the river can still be seen. In Markeaton the flow created by the two brooks was sufficient for the siting of a mill, a very valuable asset to a village in those distant days. The exact position of the Domesday mill was not recorded but we do have clues which should lead us to its site.

Once a good mill site was established, there was usually little need or reason to move it, although over many years the mill itself would have been rebuilt several times. The map shows the position quite clearly, just to the north of the hall outbuildings and at the south-east end of what is obviously a man-made dam or leat, of the type commonly constructed to create a head of water for driving waterwheels. That dam is in fact the same stream which still feeds the ornamental waterfall in the gardens and from this we can pinpoint the site of the last mill to the area by the waterfall.

This in turn leaves us with the probability that here was also the site of the Domesday mill, although, in view of the subsequent rebuilding and landscaping, it is now extremely unlikely that there are any remains to be found in the much disturbed earth to prove that particular point. At the head of the waterfall some remains of a sluice can be seen, but this is

The wheelpit of the last mill to occupy the site with the stone on which the wheel was pivoted still in situ.

The Domesday mill area at the head of the lake in the early 1930s during landscaping. The stone bridge is dated 1800 and the mill would have occupied the left side of the picture. On the right is the wooden bridge over the relief stream for the mill dam, the footings of which can still be seen. *(Derby Local Studies Library)*

One of the stone fence posts on the mill bridge. *(Author)*

made of concrete and iron and is therefore far more recent than the mill. It was probably installed to control the flow to the small waterwheel that can be seen between the waterfall and the path. This also has relatively recent origins and had nothing to do with the mill, being used to drive a pump for watering the gardens, but it does actually occupy the wheelpit of the mill. As evidence the stone bearer for the great wheel remains on the edge, although moved slightly from its original position. That this was not mentioned in the first edition of this book is due to the fact that the area was then overgrown and the stone in question was not visible, but this is typical of historical research; an old established situation is changed slightly and suddenly a piece of history is revealed.

The mill went out of use sometime between 1791, when it appeared on the second edition of Burdett's one-inch map, and 1887 when the OS six-inch map showed the bridge but no building. On the 1836 OS one-inch map a building is indicated, apparently in the correct position, but on such a small scale it is impossible to be certain that this truly represents the mill. The other remaining feature of the mill, the bridge, is dated 1800 and perhaps this tells us that this is when the mill was demolished and the bridge refurbished in order to maintain access to the rest of the park. It is an interesting thought that Constance Mundy and William Henry Fox Talbot must surely have walked over this old mill bridge during their courting days. The stream immediately to the north of the mill leat was also crossed by a wooden bridge, of which some footings remain in the water. The bridge currently in use a little to the east was built in around 1930 to replace a ford (perhaps the Roman crossing place) when the park passed into the possession of the borough Corporation.

To the west of the park, at Mackworth, were sluices to dam the brook for irrigation of the fields and traces of them can still be found. *(Author)*

Before the advent of large concrete pipes even the field ditches had to be properly bridged. It was only a little job but one done with skill and pride. *(Author)*

During the 1830s the serpentine lake created by William Emes was widened (although it was not enlarged to its present width until a hundred years later) and the stream diverted to power a paint mill on a site some way to the east, which was later redeveloped as the Britannia Mills and, until recent years, was industrially used for textile manufacture. Standing on the corner of the aptly named Mackworth Road and Markeaton Street it is currently an annexe of Derby University.

Taken *c.*1912, this shows the 'new' Mackworth Brook looking from the park to the bridge on Markeaton Lane. Postcard by F.W. Scarratt.

Confluence of the Mackworth and Markeaton brooks looking along Mackworth Brook to Markeaton Lane. Approximately the same view as the previous one. There was once a wooden bridge across the centre of this picture. *(Author)*

Some years later than Scarratt's view, this one is taken from Markeaton Lane looking in the opposite direction. *(William G. Haslam)*

Approximately the same view again today. *(Author)*

The last trace of the original brook runs from the lake on the north side and disappears under Queensway, from which point it has been completely rerouted. During that same period other changes took place in the local watercourses. Markeaton Brook changed very little apart from some straightening, but Mackworth Brook was altered in a number of places. Starting at the west end of Mackworth village, a section of the brook to the north of the castle was straightened, as was another stretch opposite the church. In the banks near here are the remains of sluices which were used for irrigation purposes and, while this may clash with the idea of flooding, to which the area seems to have been subject, it should be borne in mind that flooding was intermittent while the need for water was constant.

Not far to the west of Markeaton Lane, Mackworth Brook was straightened and rerouted to the north of its old natural course to join the Markeaton Brook in a T-junction by the Play Centre, from where it turns east to feed the waterfall and lake. A feeder from near the T-junction now takes the recut Markeaton Brook in an almost straight line to the junction of Queensway and Kedleston Road. Another cut, the Daisy Bank Branch Brook, was made and this flows to the north of the Mundy Play Centre and joins the cut of the Markeaton Brook not far from the Queensway-Kedleston Road corner, thus putting the play centre on an island. As mentioned already this land seems historically to have been liable to flooding, and these new streams must have eased that local problem, but the odd thing is that they all meet again to the east near Mackworth Road, and this must surely have aggravated an already serious situation in the town which, over the centuries, has suffered severe flooding on numerous occasions. As a result of the devastating flood which

Deceptively tranquil reflections in the park nursery garden during the floods of 6 November 2003. *(Author)*

The true picture just over the wall behind the building. The Mundy Play Centre is beyond the background fence. *(Author)*

The Green, Markeaton village during the floods of 6 November 2003. *(Author)*

Markeaton Lane. *(Author)*

submerged large areas of Derby on 22 May 1932 (caused mainly by the Markeaton Brook) the extensive flood relief culverting of these brooks was carried out later in the 1930s. This ambitious scheme actually included a tunnel to Darley Park to discharge excess water into the river there. All of this water then travelled downstream to Derby! Unfortunately parts of the scheme were never completed and on 6 November 2000 excessive rainfall again caused major flooding and Markeaton village and a large area of the park including the Mundy Play Centre were inundated.

Between Markeaton hamlet and the present Mackworth Brook is a much smaller stream, which passes almost unnoticed under Markeaton Lane and trickles toward the park. This is the original Mackworth Brook and, while it is no longer visible in the park because of the landscaping, its course is still there behind the wall of the nursery garden. Also to the west of Markeaton Lane, between the old and new brooks, the map shows a small stream. Its winding course can be seen in the grass just to the south of the present brook in a field partly occupied by a new house.

Finally, on the subject of water, there is another stream in the area which has its origins in the fields to the south of Ashbourne Road, near the junction with Prince Charles Avenue. Here a few rapidly decaying trees mark its former course. Near here was once an hydraulic ram, which was housed in a brick box with wooden doors and was built into the slope not

A few yards to the south of the present Mackworth Brook, the old one still trickles gently through the wood behind the nursery gardens to join the Markeaton Brook. *(Author)*

Another of Scarratt's excellent views showing the bridge onto the park from Kedleston Road. The Mundy Play Centre is now sited behind the bushes on the right. *(Postcard by F.W. Scarratt)*

far from where Prince Charles Avenue approaches Ashbourne Road. Its exact purpose is not known, but it was possibly used to supply water in quantity to Humbleton Farm. The interesting point about this ram is that it was invented in the 18th century by the well-known local clockmaker, scientist and inventor John Whitehurst. He would almost certainly have been on good terms with the Mundys of Markeaton, who were probably only too pleased to try the new device. Another was installed near Home Farm at Mackworth and a third at nearby Kedleston. From this wet area was cut a drainage ditch which passed under Ashbourne Road and still forms the western boundary of the pitch and putt course before, in turn, passing under Markeaton Lane by the sharp bend (as mentioned earlier in the Roman section) to join Mackworth Brook. That this stream is relatively recent is proved by the fact that it cuts across a series of cultivation strips which still continue in the field beyond.

CHAPTER EIGHT

The de Mackworth family

THE ORIGINS of this family are obscure but they appear very early on as tenants holding their land from the lord of the manor who resided at Markeaton. An account of the first six generations can be pieced together from charters published in Jeayes *Derbyshire Charters* and the *Kniveton Leiger*, although some of these are not positively traceable. The family seem by implication of the charters and the 1404 grant of arms (a combination of the arms of Touchet and Audley) to have long been in favour as stewards or senior retainers of the ancient house of Touchet of Markeaton.

In 1356 Lord Audley, Knight, distinguished himself at the battle of Poitiers in the service of Edward, the Black Prince, and one of his esquires or retainers on that occasion was a de Mackworth. The forename Robert occurs in this family, as it did in the Touchets, and, as we have already seen, Robert, priest of Mackworth, is mentioned as early as 1157 so there may be a family connection there. However, the first known de Mackworth was Philip who was alive 'very early' in the reign of Henry III (1216–1272).

Philip's son Henry occurs in the Pipe Rolls of 1254 and his (Henry's) widow is recorded as still living in 1272, while their daughter, Edith, appears in the Pipe Rolls of the same year. Edith's elder brother, Hugh, became the first prior of Breadsall in 1306. This family, like the Touchets, had their share of influence in the Church as John became vicar of Longford in 1349 and William held the living of Kirk Langley as rector from 1391–1411. The next generation produced the Reverend Prebendary John Mackworth LLD, Prebendary of Empingham, Rutland, and Dean of Lincoln,1422, but he died unmarried in 1451. He was the John to whom John Touchet, seventh Baron Audley, gave part of the estate in 1406. The Reverend John's younger brother, Thomas, married Alice, daughter of Sir John Basings of Empingham and Normanton, Rutland, and the main branch of the family may have moved

THE de MACKWORTH FAMILY.

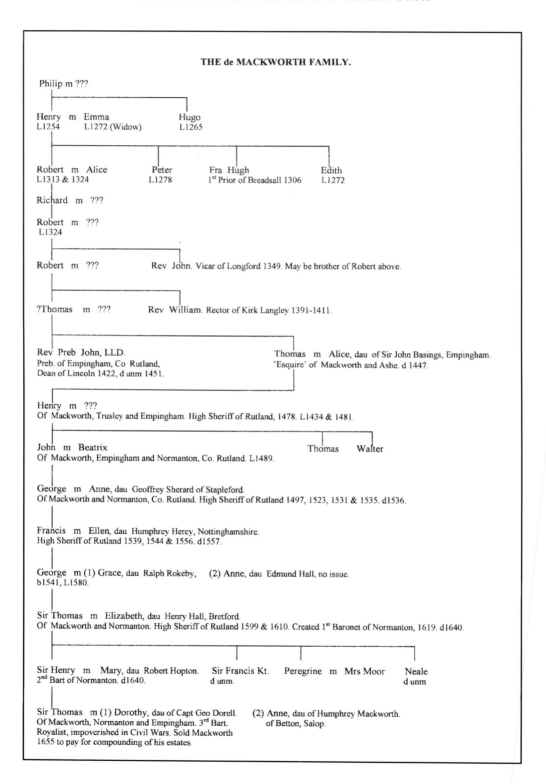

Philip m ???

Henry m Emma   Hugo
L1254   L1272 (Widow) L1265

Robert m Alice   Peter   Fra Hugh   Edith
L1313 & 1324   L1278   1st Prior of Breadsall 1306   L1272

Richard m ???

Robert m ???
L1324

Robert m ???   Rev John. Vicar of Longford 1349. May be brother of Robert above.

?Thomas m ???   Rev William. Rector of Kirk Langley 1391-1411.

Rev Preb John, LLD.   Thomas m Alice, dau of Sir John Basings, Empingham.
Preb. of Empingham, Co Rutland,   'Esquire' of Mackworth and Ashe. d 1447.
Dean of Lincoln 1422, d unm 1451.

Henry m ???
Of Mackworth, Trusley and Empingham. High Sheriff of Rutland, 1478. L1434 & 1481.

John m Beatrix   Thomas   Walter
Of Mackworth, Empingham and Normanton, Co. Rutland. L1489.

George m Anne, dau Geoffrey Sherard of Stapleford.
Of Mackworth and Normanton, Co. Rutland. High Sheriff of Rutland 1497, 1523, 1531 & 1535. d1536.

Francis m Ellen, dau Humphrey Hercy, Nottinghamshire.
High Sheriff of Rutland 1539, 1544 & 1556. d1557.

George m (1) Grace, dau Ralph Rokeby,   (2) Anne, dau Edmund Hall, no issue.
b1541, L1580.

Sir Thomas m Elizabeth, dau Henry Hall, Bretford.
Of Mackworth and Normanton. High Sheriff of Rutland 1599 & 1610. Created 1st Baronet of Normanton, 1619. d1640.

Sir Henry m Mary, dau Robert Hopton.   Sir Francis Kt.   Peregrine m Mrs Moor   Neale
2nd Bart of Normanton. d1640.   d unm.   d unm

Sir Thomas m (1) Dorothy, dau of Capt Geo Dorell.   (2) Anne, dau of Humphrey Mackworth.
Of Mackworth, Normanton and Empingham. 3rd Bart.   of Betton, Salop.
Royalist, impoverished in Civil Wars. Sold Mackworth
1655 to pay for compounding of his estates.

there as, from 1478 to 1610, they held the post of High Sheriff of that county no fewer than 10 times.

In 1619, Thomas Mackworth was created the first baronet of Normanton. He was followed by his son Henry as the second Bart and in turn by his grandson, who was the third Bart and was also an MP. This Thomas was a zealous Royalist who became impoverished in the Civil War and as a result was forced to sell Mackworth. There is a deed of conveyance, dated 1655, by which the estate passed to Sir John Curzon of Kedleston for £1,300.

The estate eventually came back into the control of the Mundys of Markeaton and, as we have seen, is still held by their successors. The baronetcy became either extinct or dormant when Sir Henry Mackworth, seventh Bart, died without issue and destitute in the Charterhouse Alms House, London, in 1803.

CHAPTER NINE

Mackworth Village

AS WE have seen earlier when considering Markeaton, the village there has disappeared without trace, except for the small hamlet outside the west gate. Landscaping, gardens and tennis courts have wiped out any sign of the mediaeval settlement. All that remains are the fossilised ridge and furrow fields and some vague shapes in the grass to the south of the hall site, the authenticity of which is very doubtful considering that this was a military training ground during World War Two and the rest of the park is still scarred by these activities. We therefore have little tangible record of the ancient village of Markeaton.

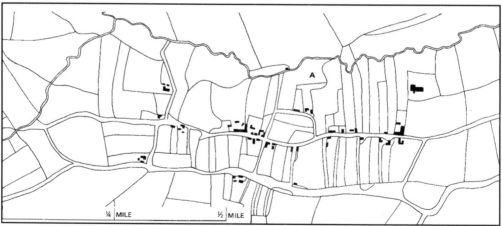

Plan of Mackworth village c.1760. Some of the buildings shown still exist, although in most cases they are somewhat altered. The long narrow crofts can be seen either side of Lower Road. A point of interest is Pinfold Lane, which is immediately below the hammer-shaped plot at 'A', a little to the right of centre on the map. (See also vertical aerial photo below and oblique photo on page 112) This area can be clearly seen from the air and also on the ground. It is illustrated in detail on pages 114–16

Vertical aerial photograph for direct comparison with the map opposite. *(Derbyshire County Council Survey, 1971)*

At Mackworth we are more fortunate in having a fairly good example of a late mediaeval settlement. The early Mackworth was partly built on a steep north-facing slope to the south of the Roman road. Exactly when the road went out of use we do not know, but to the west of the church large sections of it went under the plough as the Saxons introduced the open field system of farming with its huge areas of ridge and furrow cultivation. This resulted in the gradual formation of the two village streets winding round the edges of the village and the newly established fields. These are the present day Lower Road (formerly Town Street) and one at the top of the hill which has since been replaced by the A52 (see *Map* and section on *Roads*).

The original village would have been built of typical timber and wattle huts, infilled with clay, dung and straw, similar to those of Markeaton, and they would have required regular replacement, although by the end of the mediaeval period the standard had improved somewhat. Even so, change came slowly and, while by the 17th and 18th century more houses were being built of brick, including some very good extant local farm houses, many of the poorer ones were still little more than roofed enclosures with one or two tiny glassless windows and a hole in the roof for smoke to escape. A cottage of this crude type can be seen next to the castellated manor gateway (drawn in 1793) in the chapter on *The Castle* on page 151. In a pen and ink drawing of 1860 by Violetta Darwin, granddaughter of Erasmus Darwin, a somewhat improved single dwelling appears, while by 1868 a photograph shows this to have been replaced by a row of four tiny thatched cottages. Towards the end of the 19th century they were, in turn, altered to two, the evidence for which still shows in the blocked up doorways; at this time the thatch was also replaced with slate and in modern estate agents' parlance they are currently 'very des res'.

Mackworth Village looking north west in 1966. The Vicarage is in the centre foreground and the
A52 is on the extreme left of the picture. At 'B' are traces of the Roman road, while on either side
of Lower Road can be seen the tofts and house platforms of the early mediaeval village. This
spread gradually to the west until there was very little land to a point well beyond the 'castle' that
was not occupied at some time or other. The banks of the hammer-shaped plot are visible at 'A'
and the line of the mediaeval road can be seen at 'C'. For detail of this last feature see *Roads*,
page 88. *(Copyright reserved Cambridge University Collection of Air Photographs)*

Timber framing in Thatched Cottage. *(Author)*

Exposed panel showing the construction of
wattle and daub walling in Thatched Cottage.
The panel is about three feet wide.

Thatched Cottage on Lower Road. This once housed three families. *(Author)*

There is in the village one thatched cottage which is about 400 years old. This was originally built as two, to which, many years ago, a small extension was added, thus making it into three dwellings. It has been modernised round the original timber-framed core and still has its wattle and daub interior walls, a section of which was exposed and framed by Dr Clark-Maxwell and is kept on view. By modern standards this is a reasonably sized house, but for three families it must have been very crowded.

Each farmer would have had a dwelling according to his status, which in the case of the poorest people may have consisted of just one windowless room, possibly as small as 12 feet (four metres) square. With the cottage would have been a garden/yard for growing vegetables and perhaps keeping some livestock for food. He also had his share of cultivation strips out in the fields, allotted according to his status, where he grew his crops in conjunction with the other farmers, all working for each other. On both sides of Lower Road the remains of this village can still be seen, fossilised, as are the ridge fields around them. There are house platforms, some of which are terraced because of the slope, with their gardens to the south at the top of the hill. They can all be seen on the map as a series of narrow plots. There would probably have been no hedges, simply a narrow track or bank between them, and from the air faint traces of some of these are still visible.

In spite of the feudal power of the lords and the poverty of the peasants it should not be assumed that the situation was quite so simple. There were, of course, many grades of wealth and status between rich and poor – yeomen, businessmen and tradesmen of all classes – although it has to be admitted that the majority were at the lower end of the scale. As a result of this diversity, due to grants and sales of land many private people owned or leased land in the area and, as in modern commerce, it changed hands from time to time. This, over many years, caused the village to be gradually improved and reassembled along the two streets and from this stemmed the village of today, which, as then, is slowly but constantly changing.

Those who were fortunate enough to be able to buy their own land created plots equivalent to the number of strips they had held in the fields, and some of these may be

A beautifully executed sepia wash drawing *c.*1830–40, possibly by Laura Mundy. It shows Pinfold Lane and other features which can still be traced today. The area is detailed in the following three photographs. *(Derby Local Studies Library)*

The same view in April 1984. The drawing and this photograph are from approximately point 'A' on the inset map of 1864. The lane was on the extreme right edge of this picture where the stone-built pinfold can still be seen. The cottages stood behind the line of trees in the centre. Even the small triangular plot by point 'A' remains virtually as it was over 150 years ago. (Author)

Looking west along Pinfold Lane, April 1984. The cottages stood on the raised area to the right until they were demolished c.1930. (Author)

Looking south towards Gold Lane from point 'B' on the inset map. This overgrown hollow way, pictured in April 1984, was once a lane in regular use leading to Vicarwood and Kedleston. *(Author)*

represented on the map, but the majority of the long narrow fields abutting onto the north side of Lower Road are more likely to be the result of the enclosure awards of *c.*1760. In recent years some have had their hedges rooted out and been reclaimed as normal fields, but a few still retain their long, narrow shape. An interesting feature of this group of crofts is that most of them ended well short of the brook in an earthen bank which must have been to prevent flooding.

One particular T-shaped plot on the former Pinfold Lane near the centre of the map is still complete with surrounding banks, the height of which indicates that they were not mere fences. Also still there are the house platforms and the lanes which led to them (see a monograph by Rosemary Lucas for a detailed account of this small area. See *Bibliography.*). The cottages in the watercolour on page 114 existed till the 1930s when they were demolished along with others on the estate. Even today, with all the culverting on Markeaton Lane, these fields can become very wet in winter in spite of buried drainage. This was proved in November 2000 when the area was extensively flooded.

In about the mid-18th century, a number of yeoman farmers started building better houses for themselves. One such was Home Farm, built by the Bennett family, which is notable for the fact that it has string courses on two sides only, the ones seen from the old Ashbourne Road. Another farm, Wheathills Farm on Brun Lane, was purchased by Francis

A local family have themselves recorded for posterity in front of Mackworth House Farm, *c*.1855. The house has since been refronted and the barn on the right has gone, but anyone wishing to stand where the little boy on the left is standing, can do so. *(Derby Local Studies Library)*

Mackworth House Farm today showing the rebuilt frontage on the old house. The light mark between the upper windows is referred to in Chapter Thirteen, *Varieties,* on page 183. The line of the Roman road passes through the front garden here and under the camera position. *(Author)*

The former Church Farm on Lower Road. *(Author)*

Home Farm on Lower Road. Built *c.*1730, it was the residence of a well-to-do yeoman farmer. *(Author)*

Mundy from Richard Bateman in 1805 and over the next few years he extended and upgraded it to become a gentleman's residence. The account for this work includes the payment of £30 8s 0d to John Chatterton, central heating expert, so it was destined to have all mod cons. The total cost of the work came to £4931 10s 3½d. Since then it has had a chequered history but has, at the time of writing in April 2004, been recently lovingly restored.

Among those who at one time possessed land locally were the Abbey at Darley and Kingsmead Nunnery, which stood near Bridge Street in Derby. The Oddebroc, or Markeaton Brook, is mentioned frequently in charters and deeds relating to the Abbey. A reference to the sisters of Kingsmead appears in a grant of land dated 1549, but this was only a small part of their holdings, which included property to the west on Long Lane. The relevant part of the grant reads '... from Robert Thorley of Leighes, Co. Essex and late of Cranebrook, Co. Kent, to William Thorley, al. Draper of Mackworth, of all the lands now or lately in the occupation of Thomas Shepard, in Mackworth, late belonging to the monastery of Kingsmead, Co. Derby, now dissolved'. This tells us that the nuns' land had had at least two owners since 1536 when it was confiscated by Henry VIII (1509–1547). Back in Markeaton a charter of the time of Edward I (1272–1307) shows that some land was privately owned. It concerns a lease '... for her life, from Thomas de Derbe of Markeaton to Margaret his daughter of a place and a house standing upon it in Markeaton'. This does not necessarily mean that the land was in the village but simply somewhere in the manor which, as we have seen, was a large area.

During research for this book a request was made to the Public Record Office regarding the local tithe map as these are usually a source of useful information. The relevant part of the reply is worth quoting here. It reads, 'When in December 1846 proceedings were instituted to ascertain what tithes were to be commuted in the parish of Mackworth, it was discovered that no tithes had been paid on most of the land for many years. Much of the parish had been enclosed in 1760... but no map was found to be attached to the locally deposited copy of the enclosure award when a search was made in 1847'. Where the map was at that time we will probably never know; that it has since been recovered is beyond

Wheathills Farm on Brun Lane. It was originally much smaller, but was extended and modernised by Francis Mundy in 1805–09. *(Private collection)*

doubt as it is obviously the one reproduced early in this book. Rather surprisingly the author had a similar experience while researching these villages in the 1980s; at that time the map and the large scroll detailing the awards which should accompany it had not been recognised as belonging to each other and the scroll was issued as having no map, while apologies were later tendered for the map having no relevant information. Fortunately their connection has long since been recognised and they are now reunited. As to the missing tithes, it seems hardly credible that this situation could have occurred, but after searching enquiries this really does seem to be the case. Dr Clark-Maxwell was of the opinion that by some means or other the word 'sequestration' was applicable here. The priests of the church during this period were vicars who were not entitled to claim tithes, most of which would therefore have gone to William Mundy or even, possibly, to Derby Corporation, but as William Mundy and the Corporation were both involved in the search of 1846–47 it seems that this had not happened. What really lay behind this situation may never be known, and what is particularly puzzling is how both these parties could have been in ignorance of such an apparently long-standing clerical error. A draft tithe award was drawn up and framed in such a way 'as to prevent any question hereafter arising as to uncommuted tithes in this parish'. The three tithe-owners, William Mundy, Dorothy Trowell of neighbouring Thornhill and the Mayor, Aldermen and Burgesses of Derby all executed deeds of merger so the rent charge was not apportioned.

For most of its existence the manor consisted of three typical villages. Of these Markeaton, as we have seen, was drastically reduced by emparking, while Allestree has expanded considerably around its original core, thus obliterating many of its less substantial features under modern housing. Only in Mackworth can we be surrounded by tangible remains to remind us of its ancient origins. We know there was a Roman road and at least one Roman farmstead or villa nearby, but to what extent the area was occupied then only future investigation can tell us. Perhaps the current parish boundary is the original Roman one. Of the 'Dark Age' period we have little knowledge, but as there was a settlement at Allestree it seems a reasonable supposition that there was one here too, although to date there is no archaeological evidence to support the idea. By 1086 both villages were gone or at least reduced to the point where they were not worth recording but, as we saw earlier when discussing the Domesday entries, the reason for this state of affairs is unclear. That they recovered sufficiently to support two communities soon after Domesday is beyond question, and at Mackworth the remains of that occupation are there for all to see. Mackworth is a good example of a small village that has remained on or near its original site and is still roughly the same size as it has always been. As well as the earthworks it has an old church, the ornamental gateway to its hall and even examples of timber framing and thatching, all complemented by 1990s housing. Mackworth has definitely existed for 800 years and it could probably be as old as 1,800 years. It is to be hoped that it continues for many more years to come.

Plank bridge on the footpath to Lower Vicarwood. *(Author)*

Harvest time on a Mackworth farm in 1940. The traction engine drives a threshing machine. *(Derby Evening Telegraph)*

CHAPTER TEN

Mackworth Church

WHEN discussing the enigmatic Markeaton Church, we learned that Mackworth definitely had its own church by the late 12th century; there was certainly a church prior to the present building but for how long there had been one and where it stood is a mystery. Also under Markeaton Church we have read about the equally enigmatic priest named Robert who may well have served at Mackworth. However, as the known list of incumbents only

Threshold stone marking the end of the old path and the start of the 19th-century extension. This stone is aligned east to west with the edge of the Roman road. *(Author)*

goes back to *c.*1200, when Matthew de Touchet held the living, we must accept this as being the first positive date for a church at Mackworth.

The Roman road seems to have been used as the southern boundary for the churchyard and this situation persisted until sometime after 1851 when the church was restored and the graveyard, which was already enclosed, extended to the south. The evidence for this lies in the change of stonework in the path on the line of the Roman road and in the fact that, on the same east-west line, all the graves of pre-1851 are to the north while those to the south are all later.

The size of the early churchyard is unknown, but the 18th-century map shows it to have been much larger than at present, extending northward halfway down the field towards the brook, although it was reduced before the 1851 restoration. The old north boundary (probably only a ditch) can be seen from the air and is still traceable on the ground. The puzzle over the siting of the church is based on the old superstition that people were not buried on the north side as this was regarded as being the devil's side, yet at Mackworth the majority of the churchyard was to the north and archaeological excavation has proved the presence of burials in the field there. The siting of the church so far to the south of the burial ground is somewhat strange when we take into account the peculiar mixture of Christian and pagan beliefs which had such a profound influence on people's lives in mediaeval times. This situation, however, is not consistent and while there are churches today where burials still do not take place to the north there are others (i.e. Longford) surrounded by graves from hundreds of years ago.

The original church could have stood anywhere in this area and there is a slightly raised area to the north with stone rubble under the grass. The main possibility, however, is that it was sited where the present one stands. This idea is reinforced by the fact that in January 2006, during an excavation under the tower prior to the installation of a toilet, ancient foundations and a possible cobbled area were found. Unfortunately the excavated area was too restricted in size to ascertain what they represent and no dating material was found, but their situation surely indicates part of the early church, perhaps the base of a tower. That church would have been much

The oldest known picture of Mackworth Church, engraved in 1792. It appeared in the *Gentlemens' Magazine* in 1805 labelled as Markeaton Church. *(Private collection)*

Etching of Mackworth Church of not later than 1835 by S.F. Every. This shows clearly the former door over the parvise, the purpose of which is not known. *(Private collection)*

smaller, probably no bigger than the existing nave without the side aisles. This would perhaps explain why the chancel was built first, *c*.1320, as it could have been joined on to the old church which was later (*c*.1370–1380) replaced by the new nave, in the north-west corner of which there is some reputedly 'older stone' which hints very strongly at the new church being built onto, or with the fabric from, an earlier one.

The gap in the phases of building may have been partially caused by the Black Death, the plague which swept through the country in 1348–1351 and killed so many people. Here it is perhaps worth noting that Edmund Touscher, rector for 30 years, ceased his ministry in 1348 and that his successor, John de Folnitt, was in turn succeeded in 1352 by John de Ossewell. Did these two succumb to the plague? We don't know but there has to be a distinct possibility that such was the case. Regardless of the truth locally there is a tendency to blame the plague and its several recurrences nationally, disastrous though they were, for many things for which it was not responsible, simply because no other explanation is readily available. The desertion of many mediaeval villages throughout the country has also been credited to the plague, but archaeological and scientific investigation has shown that very few actually failed for that reason. No matter how bad the effects of the Black Death were in this part of the country, the unexplained fact remains that 28 years had already elapsed since the completion of the chancel and the arrival of the dreaded disease, although admittedly the plague may have contributed to the further delay after 1351. The most probable reason for the two separate building phases is the one given above, that the new chancel was built onto the existing nave which was not in bad condition and did not need rebuilding at that time. A third possibility is that the Lord of the Manor paid for the building of the chancel (God's half of the church) while the people were expected to pay for the nave (their half); considering their lack of wealth 60 years does not sound an excessive time for them to have achieved this but, in the end, this is all speculation and we can only guess at the truth.

The second church was built in the Decorated style but less than a hundred years later, *c*.1430–1470, the aisles, tower and porch were rebuilt, in the new fashionable Perpendicular style. This suggests that the de Touchets were maintaining their all-important social status by keeping up with the latest trend in ecclesiastical architecture, the church being a very important part of their manorial possessions and one that was very much on display. The

Photograph of 1855 after the restoration. New stonework can be seen round the top of the south aisle and the parvise as well as the blocked-up doorway over the entrance. The picture also shows the old churchyard boundary on the line of the Roman road, which was not altered for some years after the restoration. Probably by Richard Keene. *(Derby Local Studies Library)*

Letter from the Bishop of Lichfield congratulating William Mundy on the restoration of the church. The embossing at the top of the page reads 'ECCLESHALL STAFFORDSHIRE'. *(Derby Local Studies Library)*

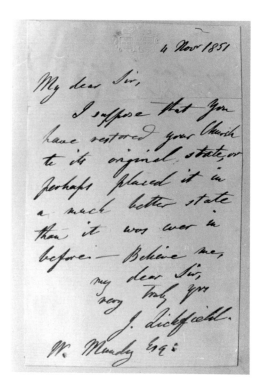

organ chamber and vestry were added in 1851 during restoration and later still the congregation were treated to the comparative luxury of heating when a boiler house was also added to the north side. The solid fuel burning boiler has been replaced by a modern oil-fired one and the whole heating system upgraded. What would our mediaeval forebears have thought of us with seats *and* heating? According to a print of 1792 the restoration included the reroofing of the south aisle, changing from a pitched roof to the present gentle slope. Excavation evidence (see *The Church Field*) indicates that the church may once have been roofed with mellow red tiles, but by 1848 a watercolour (based on an etching of not later than 1835 by S. Every, a copy of which hangs at the back of the church and is reproduced here on page 124) shows a neutral grey tone which may represent slate or lead. The idea of a lead roof comes from an unsigned handwritten note on the back of the etching, referring to Rawling's *Churches of Derbyshire* which apparently 'shows the nave with a lead roof'. An uncommon feature of the building is that the chancel and nave roofs are virtually the same height. In many old churches the chancel was built higher than the nave to show God's supremacy (i.e. at Longford and Cubley), but Victorian thinking has in numerous cases reversed this trend to make the buildings architecturally more streamlined, if less interesting.

Mackworth Church was in the hands of the de Touchets until 1497 when James was executed and attainted. The church passed to Darley Abbey and a vicar was installed by the abbot. This arrangement ceased on the Dissolution of the Monasteries in around 1536 and the church was reputedly returned to the estate via a Mr William Ragge, who had purchased the advowson from Darley Abbey. To complicate matters, as late as 1543, Robert Thacker was reputedly installed as vicar under the patronage of William Ragge's relative, Robert. Unfortunately these versions not only contradict one another, but they are also at variance with the documented one quoted earlier, where John Mundy reclaimed the advowson of the church from the enigmatic William Goche in 1516. It would be very interesting to know a lot more about Messrs Goche and Ragge and the true situation at that time. Those missing Markeaton papers could tell us so much.

In the list of incumbents which appears later in this section it will be seen that in 1662 the vicar, Samuel Ogden, was ejected. This was not for any misdemeanour but for being on the wrong side at the end of the Civil War.

Early churches were more than places of worship; they were the local meeting hall, not only for village business but for games and celebrations (strictly in the nave, of course). For this there would have been plenty of room as there were no seats other than a bench or two by the wall for the old and infirm and the family pew. In many old churches this was sited at the back, where the family would not be seen by the peasantry but from where they could keep an eye on their tenants. After the 19th century restoration the Mundys seem to have moved to the chancel; certainly Mrs Emily Mundy had her seat there.

Churches were also places of refuge in times of trouble or insurrection, during which the people and their livestock could be safe. Many mediaeval churches were fortified to some extent, but at Mackworth we have a rare, if not unique, example of ecclesiastical defensive architecture. The tower has no outside door and there are slots in the wall for a beam to secure the internal door; there are also crossbow loopholes on three sides, one of which is now obscured by the 1872 clock, and narrow spiral stairs made attack on the upper floors very difficult.

Some of the unanswerable questions this raises are: 'What was the situation that caused this ordinary little country church to require such apparently excessive fortification and

Beam slot in the tower wall. From this a balk of timber could be drawn across to secure the tower door from the inside in times of trouble. *(Author)*

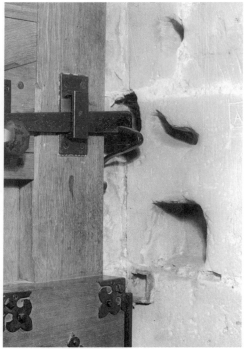

The locking slot for the beam to secure the door in the fortified tower. *(Author)*

against whom was it defended?' The physical remains we can see and examine, but what happened in and around them? It is gaps in our knowledge such as this that make us realise just how little we really do know. Although those were troublesome times, with local insurrections and skirmishes, the possibility in this case is that, once again, it may have been the Touchets, who were a powerful family locally, simply confirming their status with a touch of oneupmanship in the church.

Over the porch is a room with an unusual double squint affording a view of the two side aisles, one or both of which were probably side chapels before the Victorian restoration. Until 1851 this room had a fireplace and chimney and it may at some period have housed the priest. It may well also have served for that other use to which churches were put, that of giving sanctuary. Anyone gaining sanctuary was temporarily safe from the law and the incumbent was bound to feed and tend to the needs of those seeking his protection. There is a blocked-up doorway in the south wall of the room, which could once have led to an adjoining timber house, possibly the priest's, or there may have been a balcony from which the priest could safely speak comfort to those who were barred from the church because of leprosy or other disease. Over the porch door the position of the former projecting floor timbers can be seen where the holes have been filled with small blocks of stone. Similar blocks can be found in the sides of the tower and at other points around the church and they may represent the position of scaffolding ties during building.

For those wishing to know more about the church, the following information is based on the church guide and includes the considerable internal additions made in the latter half

Stonework over the porch doorway showing where the old floor timbers projected. *(Author)*

The church interior photographed in 1867, 10 years prior to the first of the chancel woodwork being replaced with alabaster. There are candles in the choir stalls but the rest of the church seems to have no provision for lighting after dark. *(Derby Local Studies Library)*

of the 19th century and the early years of the 20th, when the last of the Mundys lived at Markeaton Hall. Most of those additions are in Chellaston alabaster, in both the white and red veined varieties, to such an extent that the church has been described as a veritable museum of that medium. Of the superb examples the canopy over the vestry doorway is notable, as is the unique lectern, one of the church's finest possessions. These, along with the reredos, communion rails and standard candlesticks, were designed and/or created by an outstanding local craftsman, Mr Robert Gilbert Lomas, although it is probable that he

New arch to the organ chamber, created in 1851. This photograph is possibly from 1867 but certainly pre-1870 when the organ was finally installed. The print is inscribed 'The window originally between the canopies and which corresponded to that at ye east end of ye south aisle was removed and ye present arch substituted where the organ chamber were added to the church 1861'. There is a disparity of dates here, but 1851 is believed to be correct. *(Derby Local Studies Library)*

left the roughing out of the design and even some of the carving to his subordinates. In 1874 he was foreman brassfounder at Haslam's in St Helen's Street, but he changed his vocation, as he was for 12 years manager to Messrs Hall and Company of King Street, a firm of monumental masons. Later he seems to have taken over the company, as for many years into the 1920s it appears in the local directories in his name.

The South Aisle

The Touchet Tomb

In the finely moulded arched recess in the south wall is an alabaster slab, found under the floor in 1851, probably in its present position, which commemorates Thomas Touchet (Rector 1381–1409). The inscription, in Latin, is mostly worn away, but in the centre of the slab can be seen a simple cross on a stepped base and the head and fingertips of a priest.

The Piscina

The stone basin for washing the sacred vessels may have come from an earlier church. It was uncovered when the plaster was removed in 1851.

The Mundy Tomb

In brown veined alabaster, the effigy is of Edward Mundy (d.1607) and the inscription also refers to his wife, Jane Burnell of Winkburn: 'HERE LYETH EDWARD MUNDY ESQUIRE

The Mundy tomb in the south aisle dedicated to Edward Mundy (d.1607) and his wife Jane Burnell. On the side are some of their children. Carved in red/brown alabaster. (Author)

On the end of the tomb are the arms of Mundy and Burnell. (Author)

HE DYED JUNE 7 1607 AND JANE HIS WIFE DAUGHTER TO WILLIAM BURNELL OF WINKBORNE ESQUIRE 17 JUNE 1611'. On the end of the tomb are the arms of Mundy and Burnell; on the side are the effigies of their six sons and two daughters. The tomb was probably at one time in the chancel. Edward Mundy was the grandson of Sir John Mundy, Lord Mayor of London in 1522, who acquired Markeaton Hall in 1516. His (Sir John's) arms, with those of his wife Juliana Browne of London, may be seen mounted on the wall above his grandson's tomb. This tablet dates from the first half of the 17th century and may originally have been sited in Markeaton Hall. In the window above are shields which claim to be the arms of the Mundy family from the time of Edward III (1327–1377). The other senior members of the family were buried at Allestree, with the exception of Mr and Mrs F.N. Mundy, the last of the line, whose grave is outside the east window of this church.

The Green Cross
The cross on the wall above the Touchet tomb was at first a part of the Mundy memorial in the chancel.

The Windows
1. Arms of the Mundy Family.
2. With medallions of the four evangelists, 1871.
3. Scenes from the Gospels, 1870.
4. St Peter's Deliverance from Prison (Acts 12, 5–11), 1886.

The Lectern
This was given by Mrs Emily Mundy in 1903, in gratitude for 39 years of married life. Of unusual design, it is a truly remarkable feat of craftsmanship, and was carved from what was reputedly the largest single block of white translucent Chellaston alabaster ever found. It is considered to be Mr Lomas's finest piece.

The unique lectern, carved in 1903 from the largest block of white alabaster ever found at Chellaston. (Author)

The column represents the Tree of Life, with a vine spiralled round it, and at the top are grapes and vine leaves. However, the author has a friend whose great-grandfather, Joseph Norman, specialised in the carving of grapes and is believed within the family to have worked on this lectern. He was certainly a very skilled stone mason, known to have worked on other high-quality projects in Derby, and there is, therefore, a distinct possibility that this situation did occur.

The Chancel

The Vicar's Stall
With front choirstalls, given in 1934, as a memorial to Mrs Emily Mundy.

The Piscina and Sedilia
In the south wall, beyond the choirstalls, are the Piscina, for washing the sacred vessels, and the Sedilia or seats for the clergy. These date from about 1350.

Mundy Memorial
This is on the south wall and was commissioned by Mrs Emily Mundy on the death of her husband. Again, this is the work of Mr Lomas. On seeing the inscription she reputedly told Mr Lomas that she was very pleased with his work and requested that in due time, on her own death, he would do the same in the blank panel reserved for her, to which he allegedly replied, 'Madam, I shall be delighted'.

Reredos
Designed by James K. Collins and executed by Hall and Co. under the direction of Mr Lomas, the reredos was made in 1878 of Derbyshire alabaster and many other stones, mainly local but with a few imported varieties. The design was partly copied from a church at Pavia in Italy. The shield on the left bears the arms of William Mundy and his wife Harriot Frampton; that on the right, those of Francis N. Mundy and his wife Emily Cavendish. Close inspection reveals some remarkably skilled inlay work as the stones are only 4.7mm thick and very delicate. The work is signed by Mr Lomas.

The East Window
St Matthew, St Mark, St Luke and St John, 1851. The tracery, restored in 1858, is a replica of the original, which contained stained glass of Old Testament scenes.

The Standard Candlesticks
These are of unusual shape and exceptional workmanship in white alabaster. Winged angels hold the candles at the top of tall, spiralled columns. Although carved from apparently similar blocks of stone, the right-hand one is remarkably translucent when lit from behind. Date 1902.

The angels on the pair of standard candlesticks in the sanctuary. Carved in 1902 in white alabaster. *(Author)*

The right-hand angel lit from behind to show the ethereal translucent quality of the stone. *(Author)*

The Communion Rails
Of white alabaster, supported by veined alabaster inlaid with other coloured stones including Derbyshire Blue John, copied from a balustrade in Rome. Date 1893.

Canopy over Vestry Door
Dated 1886 and dedicated to the memory of Harriot Mundy. It is very finely and intricately

carved with coloured stone inlays and the angels are said to have been copied from a drawing by Corelli. The one on the right seems to be doing her best to look pleasant while supporting the weight of the pillar, while the other, with a superior look on her face, seems to be saying 'But I can do it without my hands'.

Organ and Screen
The organ chamber was added in 1851 and the organ was installed in 1870. Behind the console and painted façade pipes the rest of the instrument faces west rather than south. It appears to have been made in about 1850 and installed in the church and slightly altered in

The canopy over the vestry door, dated 1886 and in memory of Harriot Mundy. The spiral columns are inlaid with brilliant coloured stones. *(Author)*

Pencil sketch from before 1870 of a grave slab now unknown. The inscription states that it was situated 'Between chancel and organ chamber, under ye arch'. This is puzzling as the arch was not created till 1851, yet the slab looks much older. *(Derby Local Studies Library)*

1870. It is the oldest church organ in the immediate vicinity of Derby. The Iron Screen was copied from a church in Siena, Italy.

The Pulpit

This is made of Derbyshire alabaster and green Irish marble on a Dorsetshire marble base, and dates from 1876.

The North Aisle

Canopied Niches (on east wall)

Of Perpendicular period. They were moved in the 19th century from the east wall of the chancel. The arch between them was created when the organ chamber was built.

The Abbot's Seat (on north wall)

A possible link with Darley Abbey is the so-called Abbot's Seat. This canopied recess may have housed the official seat of the Abbot of Darley and was originally on the north side of the chancel. It is in late Decorated style, with some interesting carving, and bears traces of the original colouring. The lower portion appears to have been part of another memorial. The sculpture of the Madonna and Child is a replica of Michaelangelo's original in Bruges and is in memory of David Clark-Maxwell.

The Abbot's Seat. Probably removed from the chancel in 1851, this canopy may have been over the official seat of the Abbot of Darley. The statue is in memory of David Clark-Maxwell who died in 1954, aged 22. *(Author)*

Windows

1. Plain glass with some ancient fragments. The only old glass in the church.

2. Depicting Innocence, Humility and Charity in the persons of St Agnes, St Borromeo and St Elizabeth. Date 1891.

3. Plain glass (at west end). The adjacent stonework is the oldest part of the church, perhaps from the previous church.

Other Features

The Font

This is finely carved in Caen stone and dates from about 1870.

The Minstrels' Gallery

This spanned the width of the nave against the tower and the marks on the stonework show where it used to be; the position of the access door from the tower stairway can also be seen. It was removed in the 1851 restoration, when the organ chamber was added. Presumably the musicians sat elsewhere in the church for the next 20 years until the organ was installed in 1870.

The Clock

The original was made by Dent of London in 1872. Most of the mechanism was renewed in 1924 by John Smith of Derby after it had been destroyed by a weight running away. The clock was electrified in 1972 by Hartshorne of Daventry, with little alteration to the internal mechanism.

Bells

	Inscription	Weight	Bell Mark
1.	'Jhesus bee our Speed 1612'	7cwt	Henry Oldfield
2.	'God Save His Church 1616'	8cwt 2qr	Henry Oldfield
3.	'God Save the King 1662'	5cwt 2qr	George Oldfield

Registers

Dating from 1611, the church registers have mostly been deposited in the County Record Office, Matlock. Only the most recent ones are retained locally. They include a licence for an aged and weak gentlewoman to eat meat in Lent:

> Whereas the right worpll Francis Mundy of Markeaton in the parish of Mackworth and countie of Derbie Esq., for the avoiding of penalties and dangers of the laws and statutes made for restrainte of eating flesh in Lent and in consideration that he hath in his house at diett or table the right worpll Mrs

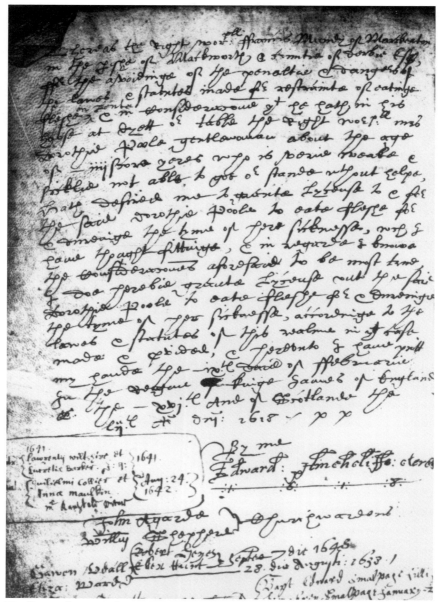

The licence for a gentlewoman to eat flesh in Lent. Dated 1618 and signed by the vicar, Edward Hinchcliffe. *(Derbyshire Records Office)*

Dorothy Poole gentlewoman about the age of four-score years who is very weak and sickly, not able to go or stand without help, hath desired me to grant license to and for the said Dorothy Poole to eat flesh for and during the time of her sickness, which I have thought fitting and in regard I know the considerations aforesaid to be most true, I do hereby grant license unto the said Dorothy Poole to

Summer 1953, a warm, balmy day showing the church in its idyllic pastoral setting. Unfortunately, nearly four years later the tree to the left of the tower fell, doing considerable damage to the north-west corner. *(Author)*

April 1957, the morning after the tree fell. The damage is being inspected by the vicar, the Revd Jack Walser. *(Derby Evening Telegraph)*

eat flesh for and during the time of her sickness according to the laws and statutes of this realm in that case made and provided, and hereunto I have putt my hand the ninth day of February in the reign of King James of England the sixteenth and of Scotland the fifty-second A.D. 1618.

By me,

EDWARD HINCHCLIFFE, Clerk *(Vicar of Mackworth, 1610 to 1638)*

Outside

The Porch

In the porch is a seat made from carved oak, perhaps part of an ancient screen, although its size and precise fit seem to indicate that it was actually designed for its present situation.

The sundial which fell in April 2001. *(Author)*

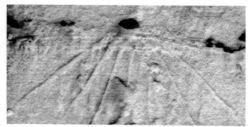

A scratch dial on a tower buttress. A stick or finger placed in the hole would indicate the time. *(Author)*

Around the church

Continuous wall plate round aisles and tower, showing they were all built at the same time. Notice the cross-bow loopholes in the tower (one hidden by the clock) and ball-flower ornaments around the chancel eaves and chancel door (these are a Victorian copy of the original Decorated work). Other notable features outside the church are mainly concerned with time, with which there seems to have been an almost obsessive interest. There was a sundial over the porch entrance, but the stone dial fell on Good Friday, 13 April 2001. The rest take the form of scratch dials; two well carved but badly worn ones are on the buttresses either side of the porch, the right-hand one bearing traces of the depressing aphorism '*UT HORA SIC FUGIT VITA HOMINIS*' – 'the life of man flies like an hour'. Three much cruder ones can also be found, one on the centre buttress of the south aisle and two on the north-west tower buttress. There is a block of stone immediately above the site of the sundial over the door bearing two parallel lines, which Dr Cox, in his *Churches of Derbyshire*, claims is part of an incised cross from an earlier church. That is a fairly bold statement, but it has to be admitted that the lines do look as if they belong somewhere else.

Although around the church there are no gargoyles, there are at the pinnacle of the spire four small stone projections which may fall under the general definition of crockets. Crockets are not rare and usually take the form of outcurving leaves or scrolls. However,

The spire of Mackworth church showing three of the four stone heads immediately below the weather vane. *(Author)*

those at Mackworth are heads and, if crockets, are rare in that form. They may even be another unique feature for this church. One opinion considers them to be possibly mid-19th century Gothic Revival fantasy, which at least explains their very good condition; a lot more wear would be expected on 15th-century work. This theory is supported by the 1855 photograph, which seems to show the top stone of the spire to be lighter in tone than the rest, thus indicating new work, and, on the south-western face of the octagonal stone, are the roughly cut initials F.A. in a rectangle. This is presumably the mason's mark and is certainly not very old. Their size is a puzzle: at a hundred feet up they are too small to be recognised without a telescope, yet the quality of the carving is very good, showing considerable pride in their creation. That these heads replace earlier ones seems likely, as elevations of the church, drawn in 1850, prior to restoration, show an indefinable 'something' in the right place at the top of the spire.

What they represent is a matter of speculation: they are possibly a hangover from pagan times and were intended to ward off evil spirits or were simply there to keep watch over the goings on in the parish – the concept of Big Brother is not new! If the latter is true then they may have failed in their purpose as the early parish records contain a list of those doing penance for fornication! Although basically human in form they are very stylised and the

The heads at the top of the spire showing at left: those on the north, west and south faces. The flat lead of the lightning conductor is 1½in wide so the heads must be about life size. At right are the west, south and east faces. The third photograph shows the mason's initials on the south-west angle. *(Author)*

The chancel doorway today, still as seen by Mrs Emily Mundy when she came to worship. (Author)

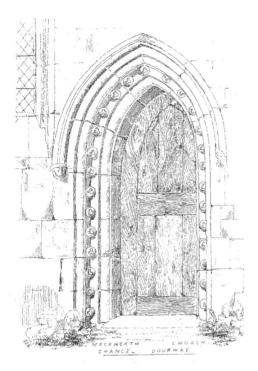

The chancel doorway before the 1851 restoration. *(Derby Local Studies Library)*

one facing north is almost animal, possibly a lion. The church is dedicated to All Saints, so could they be the four apostles? If so, one would expect a lion head for Mark, an ox for Luke, an eagle for John and a man for Matthew – and all of them winged. Are they perhaps the four winds? Both ideas are very doubtful. Are they caricatures of local people, perhaps even the masons immortalising themselves in stone for posterity? This is another unanswerable question, but it would be pleasant to think there was some humour behind those forbidding faces.

Lower down on the church there are some small carved heads, notably by the chancel door (a 19th-century copy of the earlier one) and round the pinnacles at the east end. Even graffiti have their place; on the south-east chancel buttress are some barely legible carved initials and the dates 1611 and 1614. Perhaps they commemorate members of a family buried nearby who had no other memorial. On the west face of the same buttress is a small, eroded cross and on the east wall near the Mundy tomb is a letter H, which appears to be later in style than the others. At the east end of the south aisle is a group of small circular depressions caused by musket balls; perhaps target practice took place here.

In the churchyard there are interesting memorials, including those of many local families. Under the east window are the graves of Noel and Emily Mundy and close by a long, flat stone bears the names of three former vicars, John, William and George Pickering, who between them held the living from 1731 to 1858. To the west of the church is a large, square monument with a pyramidal top dedicated to Sarah Emes, who died in infancy in December 1766. She was the daughter of William and Mary Emes of Bowbridge House (see *Varieties*). In the north-west corner, surmounted by a Celtic-style cross, is the grave of Pelham Rhodes

Ogle, vicar here from 1899 to 1904. Between his grave and the others is a space where a large tree once stood. It fell in April 1957, doing considerable damage to the north-west corner of

The boot scraper by the chancel door, probably used by Mrs Mundy and her retinue before entering the church on wet days. The scraper is of local make, probably by the village blacksmith. *(Author)*

Initials and dates on the south-east chancel buttress. Perhaps these were intended to commemorate someone buried nearby. *(Author)*

the church. Also reputedly buried at Mackworth is Edward Darwin, son of the famous Dr Erasmus Darwin, FRS. Edward lived for a while in the parish at Bowbridge House, but so far no trace of him has been found either in the parish records or the churchyard. Perhaps the saddest memorial here is a small stone in a quiet corner near the porch, dedicated to two local children who tragically died in a boating accident in 1961.

A group of visitors to the church, on seeing the number of memorials to former lords of Markeaton, were overheard remarking: 'There's more Mundy than Sunday about this place!' On another occasion some visitors were admiring the east window, which depicts the four apostles. St Matthew, on the left, holds a writing tablet and a stylus, which has the appearance of a piece of chalk or, apparently, something similar. On seeing this a child was heard to ask, 'Dad, why has that man got a cigarette in his hand?', a question which proves (if the reader will excuse the paraphrase) that you can fool all of the people some of the time and some of the people all of the time but children should be treated as a separate category altogether!

From the foregoing we know that there has been a place of worship on this site for over 800 years, possibly a lot more. It was, of course, originally a Roman Catholic church. We have seen also that the nave was the village hall, so the building was in use for a lot more than worship. We have the physical evidence, but there are many unrecorded things about which we know very little, such as the interesting question of what sort of priests and

List of Incumbents

RECTORS

*c.*1157 **Robert.** In Darley Cartulary as 'Priest of Mackworth'. Whether he was actually an incumbent is unknown.

*c.*1157 **Roger.** In Darley Cartulary as 'Priest of Markeaton'. Perhaps he was chaplain at the hall. The situation concerning these two priests is unclear. See *Markeaton Church*.

*c.*1200 **Matthew de Touchet.** There by the late 12th century. The first positively recorded incumbent.

Simon de Touchet

Edmund Touscher

John de Folnitt

John de Ossewell

Thomas Touchet

1409 **John Scot**

1409 **Thomas Holwell**

Richard Bernard

Philip More

Edward Audley. Of the Touchet family.

Thomas Toolne

H. Wryght

Edward Somer

VICARS

Edmund Lowe

Robert Thacker

William Pendleton

Hugo Cart

Edward Hinchcliffe

John Ravensdale

James Hinchcliffe

1657 **Samuel Ogden.** Ejected 1662.

James Hinchcliffe. Possibly acting during the interregnum.

Mark Hope

1649–1743 **Jasper Horsington.** Headmaster Derby School 168?–1684. Chaplain Derby Gaol.

William Laughton

John Pickering

1791 **William Pickering**

1802 **George Pickering.** Chaplain at the County Gaol and attended public executions.

William Gilder

Ascelin Spencer Perceval

Glencairn Alexander Shaw

Pelham Rhodes Ogle

Arthur Shaw Hill-Scott

William Dawes

1923 **Thomas Harding Going**

William Gilchrist Clark-Maxwell. Prebendary of Hereford.

Harold Coulthurst

Donald George Stanley Upton

Emil Jonathan Walser

Eric Parker

Edward Andrew Pratt

1979 **Henry Arthur Dane.** Priest in Charge.

Douglas Hughes. Priest in Charge.

Kenneth Jardin. Priest in Charge.

2003 **Dr Stuart Ian Mitchell.** Priest in Charge.

Revd John Pickering, born 1706, served as vicar here from 1731–1791. From a portrait attributed to Joseph Wright. *(Private collection)*

services they had all those centuries ago. Modern priests are highly trained and conform to standard service settings, but it was not always so.

There appears to have been no minimum standard in the early mediaeval days and appointment to a church was often in the hands of the Lord of the Manor. Younger brothers who had no hope of inheriting could be sent into the family church to keep all local power in the family, although unusually Thomas Touchet, rector from 1381–1409, deferred to his younger brother John, perhaps because of the latter's knighthood; the Touchets held several other senior clerical posts locally. Alternatively the appointment would go to someone in favour with the local lord. Some priests were wealthy, some lived in dire poverty; some were devout, others less so; some educated, some virtually illiterate. Few of those in country churches would have had access to a Bible, although there would have been some sort of missal or service book available; possibly some learned the services by heart and simply recited them. By the mid-16th century the chapel in Markeaton Hall possessed several old missals and psalters, both written and printed, so presumably this church was also suitably provided.

Right into the 20th century many people, especially estate workers, were expected, even ordered, to attend Sunday service regularly, although in pre-Reformation days communion was less frequent, sometimes only once a year. This would have occurred at the chancel step, the laity not normally being permitted to enter the chancel, and consisted of the bread only, the priest alone receiving wine. The altar rail was a later innovation.

An important part of most modern services is music. By the 12th century abbeys and cathedrals were singing parts of their services, but less is known about the smaller churches. This one had a minstrels' gallery, but when it was installed we do not know.

After the Reformation, when Henry VIII declared himself head of the English Church, the situation gradually evolved to what we have in our various churches today. Gone are the days of a priest advertising for a post in a country parish with 'light duties and plenty of sport' or announcing that 'Divine service will be held at least three times a year.' There is much talk today about declining congregations, but if attendance at church had always been voluntary how big would the congregations have been?

From the above description the reader will realise that this church, listed by English Heritage as Grade I*, is truly a quite exceptional and unique building. It was, for hundreds

Photograph of the old Mackworth vicarage, 1870, superseded in 1879 by the present building which is now a private house. *(Derby Local Studies Library)*

Another view of the old vicarage. *(Private collection)*

In 2001 a charitable trust, the Friends of All Saints, was founded. Their first fund-raising function was a car boot sale in August of that year. *(Author)*

of years, maintained and improved largely at the expense of the lord of the manor, but those days are over and now, in common with many other parishes, it relies on the fund-raising efforts of the parishioners. As All Saints now serves a very much reduced congregation, it in consequence receives an equally reduced income. Unfortunately, fabric deterioration is a continuous process which needs to be matched by regular maintenance, and in order to help preserve this historic gem, in August 2001 a charitable trust, The Friends of All Saints Church Mackworth, was set up to raise funds. At the time of writing in August 2005 the trust is four years old and, through a series of events and hard work, is steadily raising much-needed money.

CHAPTER ELEVEN

The Church Field

EARLY Mackworth may have been a cluster of cottages round the church, there being no hall or manor house in those days. This theory, of course, depends on the origins of the church, which have already been discussed. There are certainly slight signs of habitation in the field round the present churchyard, along with the fairly obvious remains of the agger, or embankment, of the Roman road, all of which shows how careful we must be in making such assumptions, as excavation has shown that things are not quite as they seem. In 1979–80 R. Cowell of the then Trent Valley Archaeological Research Committee (now Trent and Peak Archaeological Trust) did a general visual survey of the area which indicated that these remains (which are mostly very slight) are house platforms with associated ditches and banks. Surprisingly, he omitted the Roman road from his survey. His report was published in the Derbyshire Archaeological Journal, Vol. C1, 1981. That same year the Archaeological Research Group did a physical survey to establish the size and shape of the mounds and also the section of the Roman road which appears as a low but distinct ridge both to the east and the west of the churchyard. Probing established the presence of hard material very near the surface in both places, with stone projecting from the grass at one point. In October 1981 the section to the east of the churchyard was excavated.

A trench was planned north to south across the alignment and the turf removed. This revealed not Roman road, but quantities of orange-red tile, which may well have come from the roof of the church at some time and had presumably been used for remetalling. This route was in regular use over many years, right into the 20th century, and is still a popular footpath today. Below the tile material were sandstone blocks, set in gravel, arranged as a kerb, while nearby stone sets were found, bedded in small pebbles and gravel. Other finds included small quantities of Romano-British Derbyshire ware, a coarse type of domestic pottery, and post-mediaeval glazed ware. This was a far from perfect specimen of a Roman road but, as any form of building material was always in demand, it is somewhat fortunate that even this much remained to show where the road used to be. Perhaps the fact that it had not been too badly disturbed was due to its being in the old churchyard. There may also have been a cottage on the site at some time; the ready-made floor would have been very welcome and, as it was on a raised area, there would have been no drainage problem.

In April 1982 the equally obvious agger of the road to the west of the churchyard was similarly treated. Obvious in appearance it certainly was, but that was where the similarity ended. Apart from a scattering of stone near the surface nothing was found except a small quantity of burnt lead, possibly from window glazing. The ground had been much disturbed and whatever had been there was gone, with the result that this dig lasted less than a day. Fortunately, the close proximity of the road to the east of the churchyard, along with other traces in the fields to the west, confirmed that this site was on the original alignment.

The early failure of this second dig prompted some members of the group, who were then surplus to requirements, to investigate the low mounds to the north of the church. Dowsing and probing suggested, among other things, a rough rectangle of stone under the grass. A small exploratory dig a few weeks later showed this to be a scattering of sandstone rubble, which is not surprising as the church has, over the centuries, had much work done on it and the stonemasons must have worked somewhere. That the rubble really is in a rectangular area has yet to be proved, but there is the possibility that it may have been used as the base for a timber building of more substantial proportions than usual, such as a tithe barn.

Another dig during a very hot weekend in August 1983 also revealed signs of habitation in the form of laid pebbles and shards of mediaeval pottery. However, the most interesting feature of these two digs was the discovery in the first one, less than two feet under the rubble, of the burial of a small male in a grave aligned east to west and, in the second, remains which indicated another grave, although the ground had already been disturbed in the past. As the remains were not removed their age is as yet uncertain. Dowsing indicated more graves in the area, but they have been left undisturbed. The only positive conclusion to be gained from these finds is that whatever buildings may have stood in the then churchyard came after it had been originally established as a graveyard. This is not unlikely as graves were mainly unmarked and churchyards, and churches, were treated much more as common property than their modern counterparts. It is therefore quite possible that buildings for domestic or storage purposes were sited near the church at some later period.

Much more work will be necessary to show the true sequence of occupation, but all of this is for the future. How far into the future is a moot point, as policies have changed and there is not a lot of encouragement for amateur groups to excavate without very good reason, as it is considered better to leave sites untouched for the advent of new techniques and equipment. Without digging we already know that much of this area has been disturbed, as a photograph of 1855 shows large trees not far to the north of the church and their roots must have done extensive damage to whatever was under the grass. Nonetheless, it is hoped that investigation will continue in due course.

To the south of the churchyard is a crescent-shaped depression in the field, which may once have been a fishpond. A mid-19th century watercolour shows a small area of this pond

The crescent-shaped depression to the south of the church that may have been a fish pond. It still seasonally contains water. *(Author)*

with reeds growing along the bank. The first map seen by the author which shows this feature is the OS one-inch map of 1836, although it must be much older. However, apart from the earth banks to the south, the other features found during Cowell's survey are very difficult to distinguish and to see them, according to one archaeologist, requires a lot of experience and the eye of faith. It is still quite probable that at some distant time much of the village was sited here, but the simple cottages were so insubstantial that they would have left no trace other than post holes and even those would not have survived the ground being disturbed. The only fact which seems fairly certain is that the field has never been ploughed.

CHAPTER TWELVE

The Castle

THE DE Mackworth family lived in a building, now gone, but locally remembered as The Castle. The farm which occupies the site is known as Castle Farm. The OS two-and-a-half inch map refers to 'Castle, remains of' and in those brief statements is embodied practically all the evidence there is for a castle at Mackworth. Of course it all stems from the stone gateway which is such a prominent feature on Lower Road and which, at first glance, may suggest the former presence of a castle. A second glance soon dispels any such fanciful thoughts. The gateway has been dated to *c.*1495–1500, which seems in any case to be rather a late date for castle building in this area. It is crenellated and buttressed, but examination shows it to be too lightly built to have ever been intended for serious defensive purposes. Even more to the point is the fact that it was built as a three-sided stone shell; the back wall, if it was ever installed, would have been timber-framed, a feature that was hardly conducive to internal security. Also it has three large windows on the front and one on the east end, something rarely found on a building designed to keep unwelcome visitors out! There is decoration in the form of gargoyles and small carved heads. The roof and the north inside wall have gone, but what remains shows a fireplace (now bricked up) on the upper floor with its attendant chimney and traces of a corner spiral staircase.

The building was probably originally intended to be a rather ornate lodge, with the gatekeeper's dwelling over the gateway. If the dating of this structure to a little after 1495 is correct then it could coincide with the end of the de Touchet family at Markeaton in 1497, and it is therefore possible that this was the first stage of a refurbishing or rebuilding of the de Mackworth seat to bring it up to the standard required to match the status of people who suddenly found themselves the senior local family. That the project was apparently not completed could be due to their having found even greater status in Rutland (George de Mackworth was already High Sheriff of Rutland in 1497) and their subsequent move away from Mackworth soon after it was started.

The oldest known picture of the gateway, engraved by Malcolm in 1793. Note the cottage on the right as mentioned in the text on Mackworth Village. *(Private collection)*

A charming pen and ink sketch of 1860 by Violetta Darwin, granddaughter of Erasmus, which shows the cottage substantially improved. *(Derby Local Studies Library)*

The gateway seen from the west in 1867. The turret seen slightly to the left of the entrance is a chimney. The cottage has been replaced by a row of four which still have thatched roofs. *(Derby Local Studies Library)*

An 1890 photograph by Richard Keene showing little alteration to the gateway but dramatic change in the cottages. The thatch has gone, the roofline has been raised and the roof newly slated. A blocked doorway (behind the bush on the left) tells us that four rather cramped dwellings have been combined into two reasonably sized ones. *(Derby Local Studies Library)*

The remains of the fireplace in the gatehouse.
(Author)

It would not be fair to dismiss the idea of a castle without at least considering what little information there is, but it must be emphasised that there is, to date, not one item of actual historical evidence to support that idea. Physically there are no remains whatsoever, nor is the amount of stonework in nearby buildings of any significance; there was plenty of that available, although it cannot be denied that some of this may have come from the site. A little to the west of the gateway, in a field by the lane, are two large house platforms. One gentleman, writing in the late 19th century, was quite emphatic that these mounds were typical castle courtyards. What he failed to mention was that, if this was correct, the demolition of the supposed castle must have been so total that not one single stone remained, nor was any trace left on (or in) the ground of where the presumably substantial foundations must have stood. Even on the site of the huge Norman keep at Duffield, which was deliberately dismantled before the year 1300, the foundations still remain, showing walls sixteen feet (4.8m) thick.

In the field immediately to the north of Castle Farm is the large platform on which the manor house stood. Nearby are more building platforms, all of which tie in with the notion of a mediaeval manor house of timber and plaster, possibly on a stone foundation similar to Markeaton, with its attendant outhouses and barns. The siting of the house is interesting in that its relationship to the Roman road, the line of which crosses Lower Road a short distance to the east of the gateway, is similar to that of the church, which indicates that the road was still in use when the de Mackworths first came to live here. In *Magna Britannia* Vol. V (1817) the brothers Lysons refer to a 'castellated mansion' at Mackworth, but they give no hint as to where this information originated and we can only presume that they saw the gateway or perhaps a picture of it and made the wrong assumption. Even they, whom historians generally accept as being very careful and accurate in their research, in the same book referred to the manor house at Norbury some miles to the west as being 'long gone', while it is actually still standing as the oldest secular building for many miles around, thus showing how easy it is to fall into error when dealing with history.

Oliver Cromwell gets a dishonourable mention, at least in local legend, for destroying the castle. His local troops reputedly bombarded it with cannon placed on the hill to the south and this has appeared on some maps as Cannon Hill. If there is any historical truth in this then his gunners must have been remarkably inept, as the gateway shows no scars of battle, yet we would have expected it to have been badly marked if not totally destroyed. It has to be admitted as a possibility that Cromwell's troops may have razed the house to the ground, but there is no actual evidence or record of such an incident and in the absence of excavation this point is not likely to be resolved. The author has been shown one small

Photographed by the gateway *c.*1886–87, this young man was well in fashion for mobility with his Penny-Farthing bicycle. Assuming, of course, that he could ride it! *(Private collection)*

cannonball and a number of musket balls found locally but these are insufficient to prove that any substantial conflict occurred here.

There was no castle nor is any other house historically recorded as being destroyed in

anger. A far more credible end to it is the idea of the local people making use of a lot of good timber and stone from a decaying ex-family residence for which the distant owners no longer cared. This was the fate of other timber-framed houses not too far away at about this time, notably Sharrow Hall at Thurvaston and Cubley Hall. The estate was sold in 1655 and most reports vaguely seem to assume the house to have been in ruins by that date, if there was anything left at all, although there is no mention of its condition in the deed of conveyance.

This attractive young lady stands in the doorway of the cottage next to the gateway. It seems to be used as a shop as the notices inform us that Sturgess and Co.'s Mineral Waters and Fry's Chocolate are available here, as is hot water for picnic flasks.

CHAPTER THIRTEEN

Varieties

IN THE first edition this chapter was entitled *Miscellania,* but as it now contains more items from Mrs Emily Mundy's own book *Varieties,* and as she is mentioned in the following pages, the heading has been changed as a compliment to her. In these final pages we have a brief look at the multitude of items of interest, the people and some of the changes that have taken place that do not readily fall into any particular category so far discussed. As an example, education is in here, as it applied to the whole estate rather than the separate villages. This is therefore the longest chapter.

A great deal of information comes from place and field names, as they often give a clue to local activities and ownership in years past, or they may indicate the type of land in a given area. Humbleton, away on the south edge of the manor, was, until the mid-1950s, a thriving farm. The name Humbleton may mean 'rounded hill', which is quite reasonable if one imagines the site without houses. In this instance the 'ton' part of the name does not describe a settlement but is a corruption of 'dun', the Old English for a hill, and many places nationwide derive their names from this source. Another local example is Bupton (now in Longford) or Bubba's Hill. Some names are more obvious, and Bowbridge on the Ashbourne Road needs no clarification as to its origins, which date back to at least 1306 when it was referred to as 'pontem inter Makworth et Langel' or 'bridge between Mackworth and Langley'. Windmill Hill Lane, the old road from Derby to Radbourne, passes through the southern part of the manor.

This would have been the route taken by Bonnie Prince Charlie on his way into Derby after his conference at Radbourne Hall. Again there is no need to say why this road is so named. It actually had two mills; one, which appears on the 1791 edition of Burdett's one-inch map of Derbyshire, stood in the angle between the lane and Ashbourne Road and another, a 19th-century one, was a brick-built tower which stood until the early 1970s near Station Road at Mickleover, although this one was never in the manor and also, of course, came far too late to influence the naming of the lane. Brun Lane passes through an area which was once Brund Common, and from this we learn that the land concerned was probably cleared many years ago by burning, a system of land clearance which dates back to Neolithic times.

In the early days the manor had large, open fields, each divided into many groups of furlongs intermixed with areas of pasture and woodland. The original fields at Markeaton were named Vicarwood, Lowhill, Ironer and Church fields, while those at Mackworth were named Highgreave, Brook and Brund fields. Gradually these were sub-divided until, after the enclosures of *c.*1760, there were well over a hundred fields in the manor, each with its own name and in some cases a story behind the name.

While the origins of many field names are obvious and others can be traced we are left with some which appear obvious but are not, and still others which seem to defy explanation. One quaint name, The Dumble, is actually quite common in the south of the county. It derives from the Old English *dympel*, meaning a deep hole or pit, a word which still survives today as dimple, although its meaning has been modified. Hanging Furlong has no connection with the gallows which once stood hereabouts, but refers simply to a sloping field.

The influence of the church is also evident in some of the local names. Abbot's Meadow is a reminder of the fact that Darley Abbey held land here, while Parson's Close and Priestwood speak for themselves so far as ownership is concerned. Vicarwood seems equally obvious, but is deceptive, being derived from Bikerwode, Beekeeper's Wood. The nuns of Kingsmead are remembered by the field name Nunpit. What they got from the pit we do not know for sure, but three more names give us a clue; they are Stonepit Furlong, Gravel Pit Wood and Markeaton Stones. Much of the land is indeed very stony and there are still fields bearing traces of gravel extraction. Also layers of natural gravel were clearly shown in 1980–81 when Markeaton Lake was drained for cleaning and the strata could be seen in the bank.

Gosling Close leads to the thought that here could be a direct connection with the founder of the Touchet family, Gozelin or Jocelyn. Regretfully this is not based on fact. The word gosling is a quite recent form of *goslon*, which in turn is derived from *gosland*. This seems to infer the place where the village geese were taken to forage and therefore gosling may, accidentally, be nearer the literal truth than any fanciful thoughts of Gozelin, attractive though this original idea may be. Dough Meadow may indicate very soft, moist ground but the origins of Ironer Close, Foul Seller and Short Woollen Bed stretch the imagination somewhat! Gold Lane has been cut through to reduce the slope for vehicles as it would have been very steep. Why it is so named we do not know; perhaps it was once Cold Lane or Old Lane. Dialect does strange things to words and, as an example, at Little Eaton the Old Lane has changed through T'owd Lane to Toad Lane and finally, according to the OS map, Todd Lane, although the name plate still says Toad Lane. Because of dialect there may never have been a Mr Jarvey in Mackworth, as there used to be a Jowis Lane and it needs but little imagination to effect the change.

This photograph of *c.*1928 shows, in the foreground, Kingsway under construction near Thornhill House. The tall white post to the left of centre is a railway signal on the LNER line, while the fields in the distance are now covered by the Mackworth Estate. *(Derby Museum and Art Gallery)*

Another feature of field names is the frequent reference to brick-making. Most villages had to be self-sufficient and in the clay lands in the south of the county brickyards were common. Some were large and well-established while others were only temporary affairs set up to build one house or a perhaps a farm. Allestree had one opposite the end of Allestree Lane and this site was later known as Brickyard Pasture. It was from here that the last Markeaton Hall was created. Not far away, towards Darley, two fields bore the names Nether and Far Brick Kiln Close, while over on the southern boundary with Radbourne is Brickyard Wood. There were also clay pits near the Rowditch, next to Thornhill Farm, which developed and, until the 1950s, existed as Derby Brick Works. There was a large circular kiln with deep entrances which were much sought after by vagrants on winter nights. When worked out this area became a landfill site and it is currently occupied by a number of superstores. A couple of old bricks, presumably of the 18th century, from Markeaton Park, are considered to be of local manufacture and appear to be of the type used in the last hall which was built in 1755.

After World War Two new housing estates were built which wiped out a large number of fields. One, the Markeaton Estate, to the north of Kedleston Road, joins through to Allestree to the extent that it is now considered to be part of Allestree and has long since lost its original title; as a result many people are not aware that it was ever so-called. Some of this housing obliterated part of the Markeaton Golf Course. The campus of the former

This 1950s view shows Thornhill Farm and a little to the right the square chimney stands in the centre of the circular kiln of Derby Brick Works. The whole of this area has disappeared under the Kingsway retail complex. *(Author)*

1930s aerial view of the Derby Brick Works showing the circular kiln. In the middle distance is the new Morley Estate with the white line of the recently built Kingsway at extreme top left. *(Derby Museum and Art Gallery)*

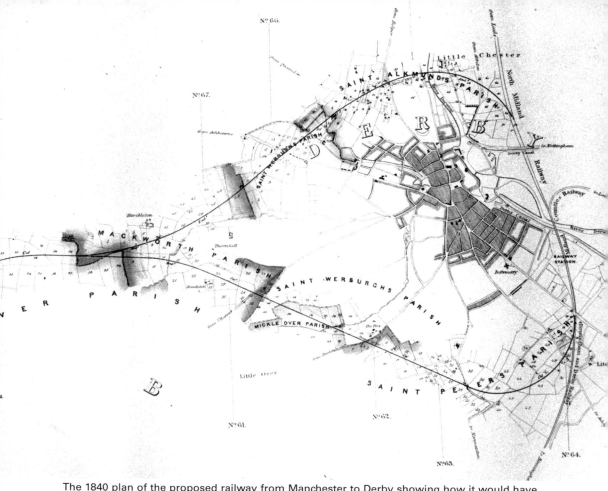

The 1840 plan of the proposed railway from Manchester to Derby showing how it would have approached Derby station from two directions. The point where the line divides is almost exactly where the east end of Mickleover tunnel was built 35 years later. In spite of its name the tunnel is partly in Mackworth parish. *(County Record Office)*

East end of Mickleover tunnel in January 1983 before it and the cutting were filled in. *(Author)*

Derby Colleges of Art and Technology, now ennobled to the rank of Derby University, also occupies a large area to the north of Kedleston Road, much of which belonged to the Markeaton Golf Club. This club house could, until fairly recently, also still be seen close to Maxwell Avenue.

The other new estate, Mackworth Estate, lies to the south of Ashbourne Road and stretches to the boundary with Mickleover. This estate overran the ancient site of Humbleton, which is now commemorated by no more than a street name and Humbleton View Day Centre. Part of this area was once home to the Derbyshire Golf Club and an OS map of 1913 clearly indicates a Golf Course and a Club House. Twenty years later an aerial photograph shows the house surrounded by farmland without any trace of a golf course. During World War Two some of these fields between Ashbourne Road and Kingsway vanished under military occupation, with a large anti-aircraft battery being sited there. After the war the area was covered by much-needed housing, in the midst of which the Club House still stands, now in residential use.

In 1878 the southern part of the manor was cut off from the rest in a very positive manner. This was caused by the coming of the Great Northern Railway and a deep cutting was made to accommodate it which, near Mickleover, led into a quarter-mile long tunnel. The railway had existed for just 90 years when the last train ran in 1968 and the track was subsequently removed. Its closure and the infilling of the tunnel with thousands of tons of refuse has resulted in a nature reserve being created. Unfortunately, the concurrent infilling of one of the bridges which formerly connected Humbleton Farm with its fields has badly restricted drainage and the floor of the cutting is now an uninviting, overgrown swamp, which has nonetheless developed to become the ideal habitat for numerous varieties of flora and fauna. It also appears to have a magnetic attraction for supermarket trolleys, old motorcycles, washing machines and the like, plus the occasional burnt-out car. This seems to be the price of living in an age of mass-produced rubbish; how would we manage without redundant railway cuttings, quarries and the like?

On the subject of railways, in her diary for 1846 Mrs Harriot Mundy had noted that 'Surveyors are wishing to survey for a railroad from Derby to Ashbourne. They are composed of English, Scotch, Irish and French'. Was this the same railway which had been formally planned and submitted for approval in 1840 and had appeared in the *Parliamentary Gazetteer* parish reports for 1843–44, where Mackworth was '…in the line of the projected Manchester and Derby railway'? Perhaps the 1846 one was a later proposal. From Manchester the proposed 1840 line went south via Ashbourne and Rocester, then turned east roughly parallel with, and south of, Long Lane till it divided very near where the much later Mickleover tunnel was built. The northern route passed close to Humbleton Farm and crossed Ashbourne Road, right through where the Wagon and Horses now stands near Windmill Hill Lane, before cutting across to Little Chester and joining the main Midland line near St Mary's Wharf. The southern branch cut through Mickleover and Normanton to join the main line south of Derby Station. This project did not come to fruition and its failure was followed in 1882 by that of a proposed branch line from the

Vine Cottage, which stood on Markeaton Lane on the site of the crematorium car park. The cement facing concealed a much older building, which may have been timber-framed. It narrowly missed demolition during World War Two when a bomb landed in the wood a few yards away. *(L.F. Litherland)*

Near Markeaton Lane can be seen the water-filled trace of the bomb crater which so nearly destroyed Vine Cottage. *(Author)*

newly opened Great Northern Railway near Radbourne and again in 1901 by plans for a light railway which would have run close to the present A52. A bus service started between the two towns in 1909. A final word on the subject of transport. In the mid-1930s an airport was planned for Derby and the first site proposed was on land to the west of Radbourne Lane, spilling over into Mickleover on the present football ground and Radbourne Gate residential estate off Station Road. There were many objections and eventually the airport materialised at Burnaston, being opened in 1939.

Apart from the hamlet at Markeaton there were, on or outside the park boundaries, cottages for keepers and other employees of the estate. When, in the early 1930s, the Revd W.G. Clark-Maxwell inherited the estate, about 30 such dwellings were derelict or in very poor state of repair. These were all demolished, the inhabited ones being replaced with new houses. One such stood by the entrance to the 'side gate' on Ashbourne Road and prior to World War Two the tiled floor could still be seen. Another, Vine Cottage, was at one time the residence of the butler from the hall. It stood on Markeaton Lane until the laying of the crematorium car park, which now occupies the site, although a variety of red-leafed cherry tree from its garden still survives near the gate. This one narrowly missed premature destruction during the last war when, in January and June 1940, German planes, presumably aiming for the army base on Markeaton Park, dropped bombs between Humbleton and Quarndon and two fell only a few yards from the cottage, killing three cows in the next field. A third bomb fell near Stones Farm, damaging windows and punching a hole in the garden wall, which is still there as a reminder of the event.

Markeaton Stones Farm, which narrowly missed destruction in World War Two when a stray bomb landed in the adjacent field. Windows were blown in but otherwise the house escaped with little damage. *(Author)*

The garden wall at Stones Farm showing a hole blasted through the brick by flying shrapnel. *(Author)*

A very small dwelling, Rose Cottage, also stood on Markeaton Lane near Ashbourne Road while others were on Kedleston Road opposite Maxwell Avenue, Windmill Hill Lane and Peel Street when that area was still open fields, a situation which is difficult to imagine now. All have been demolished. A large house of *c.*1760 in Markeaton (pictured on page 82) was removed in the 1960s and the site is now a nursery garden.

Another tiny one-up, one-down house on Ashbourne Road in 1928 (right). It was removed in the 1960s. *(Derby Local Studies Library)*

(Above) Cottages on Kedleston Road, which stood nearly opposite the entrance to the University. They were used as a Toll House until a new one was built nearer to Markeaton Lane. They were demolished in the 1940s. *(Derby Museum and Art Gallery)*

(Left) Mrs Needham's cottage on Windmill Hill Lane in 1895. Typical of the dwellings built around the estate when Markeaton Village was cleared in the 18th century, it was demolished in 1911. *(Derby Museum and Art Gallery)*

Rose Cottage on Markeaton Lane, sometime pre-1914. Even this tiny dwelling was once half the size shown. The left half is original and was thatched. The bricks over the far upper window show that the roofline was raised for tiling, possibly at the same time the extension was added to the right.

On Lower Road in Mackworth stands a small, single-storey cottage. This was the local school until 1868 when William Mundy, who was something of a perfectionist, erected an ornate and well-built replacement across the road. This was a mixed school designed for 100 pupils, but it is doubtful whether it ever saw that number at one time. It did, however, indicate a change towards a more liberal attitude to education. The first indication of education in the area was in 1815 when Joseph Gorse was recorded as 'Schoolmaster'.

Peel Street, Derby. This cottage, dwarfed by late Victorian housing, is typical of the type of dwelling erected on waste land during the latter half of the 18th century and the early 19th century. Along with others, now lost, it may have been built as a direct result of the emparking of the village at Markeaton. It has now been demolished. *(Author)*

Mackworth's first school, now a private residence. *(Author)*

The newly built Mackworth School on Lower Road in 1868. *(Author)*

The school building in 1984, somewhat altered but still easily recognisable. The road surface is also somewhat improved. *(Author)*

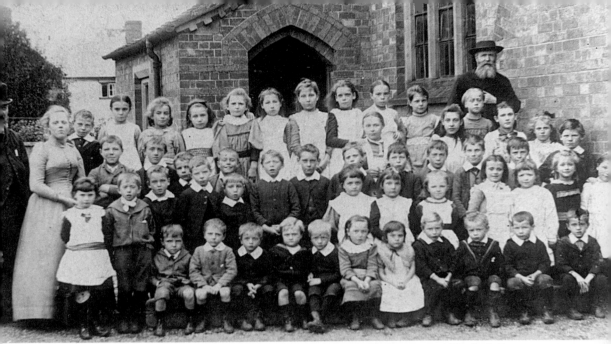

Mackworth school *c.*1891. This shows, on the left, husband and wife George and Elizabeth Dutton, who ran the local schools for 42 years from 1866 to 1908. At the back on the right is Richard Keene, Derby's first professional photographer, appearing in yet another of his own photographs. This one was actually taken by his son, Charles Barrow Keene. *(Richard Keene)*

On Markeaton Lane was a pair of semi-detached, one up, one down type of labourers' cottages, built perhaps in the mid-18th century. At some point these two cottages were knocked into one and a schoolroom built on the end. This served as a house for the schoolmaster and his wife and also as a classroom for girls, where they spent the afternoons learning the practical skills of sewing, embroidery and the like. The room extended to the full height of the house and was furnished with plain wooden desks on a stone floor. There was a stove for heating but it would still have been rather cold in winter. The boys remained at Lower Road, where they were taught woodwork and other skills. Spartan though these schools were, it was a very welcome move towards the better education of the local working-class children and they were probably no worse off than many of their contemporaries if Charles Dickens's accounts are anything to go by.

The teachers were husband and wife George and Elizabeth Dutton, who were in charge of education here for 42 years from 1866 until their retirement in 1908. He ran the mixed school while she supervised the girls' establishment. Mr Dutton combined

Old School House on Markeaton Lane. The far end was formerly two cottages and the schoolroom was added *c.*1868. *(Author)*

his profession with that of assistant overseer on the estate, collector of taxes and choirmaster. He died in November 1916 and 13 days later his wife was laid beside him in Mackworth churchyard. The school for girls ceased on the retirement of the Duttons and is now private houses. The mixed school on Lower Road was in use for about a hundred years until it eventually closed in favour of the mass education machines now so popular with local authorities, but has fortunately found a new lease of life as the church hall. Also within the manor there was a private fee-paying school on Radbourne Lane, known locally as the Academy, which still stands not far from Ashbourne Road. The old schools may be gone, but education continues locally with schools and a college of higher education on Mackworth Estate, while nearby the concrete and glass bulk of Derby University towers over Kedleston Road, from where it can be seen from practically every point of the manor.

In August 2005 the author was given three volumes which had been rescued from a derelict outbuilding attached to some cottages which were to be demolished. They were written by Master Frederick W. Haynes of Mackworth School in 1863. The books carry the title *A Collection of Arithmetical Questions* and are immaculately handwritten, with decorative title pages drawn and lettered with considerable skill. Who Frederick was is a mystery, as is the identity of the school, although the title page does tend to indicate the village school. In those days the word 'Master' referred to someone under 21; he was not the village schoolmaster as James Chivers held the post prior to the Duttons. No man of that name appears in any relevant census up to 1901 nor in the church records until 25 March 1897, when *a* Frederick William Haynes attended the adult baptism of his daughter Louisa, at which time he was listed as a labourer. We do not even know if this is the same man and it is hard to reconcile such delicate artistic talent and mental ability with a life of manual labour.

The books contain examples of many problems on subjects such as Inverse and Compound Proportion, Mechanics and Hydrostatics, Duodecimals and Commission and Brokerage. The 'Three R's' taught at day school certainly did not include arithmetic of this level. As an example, one page is taken up by a long multiplication which ends with the answer of 11 and a fraction worked to 18 decimal places. The subject matter does seem to be far in advance of what the average 1860s village child could have expected to be taught (and 80 years later when the author was at junior school level!) and the thought arises that perhaps they were written to be used in classes where the academic level was somewhat higher. We must not forget that while the education of local children may have been limited compared to modern standards, the latent academic potential must surely have been there and adult classes would have been a natural progression for those who wished to improve themselves. Did he study at evening classes, perhaps working towards some qualification? And, *if* the labourer above is the same man, what happened to frustrate such talent?

Along with the three books came another, the bound volumes of *The Cornhill Magazine* for 1872. The main point of interest here is that inside the cover is a sticker declaring that the book belonged to the Markeaton Lending Library, which emphasises the fact that there was a move to wider interests and academic improvement for the working classes. A penny

Markeaton island in 1933, when there was slightly less traffic congestion than today! At the left stands Markeaton Hill Farm, which was demolished the following year. *(Derby Industrial Museum)*

fine was to be paid if the book was damaged or dirtied and at the end were the initials E.M., which dates it to the time Emily Mundy was lady of the manor (1877–1929).

Not too many years ago another important feature in any rural village was the pinfold, where stray animals were impounded until reclaimed by their owners, at a price. The one at Mackworth still exists as part of a private garden but, like the village schools, it is a thing of the past. Also gone is the animal water trough on the corner of Gold Lane and Ashbourne Road. These were also a common feature in towns where most of the traffic was horsedrawn.

On the Ashbourne Road are the village's two hostelries. The Mackworth Hotel, an old but much modified house, was for a while in the 19th century home to Henry Isaac Stevens, the noted local architect, and in the 20th century the last family to occupy it were the Clark-Maxwells, the heirs to the Mundy estates. In a garden opposite the Mackworth Hotel is an old railway carriage, a former Family Coach which could be hired privately and attached to the appropriate train for an exclusive day out.

A short distance to the west is the Mundy Arms Hotel, until the mid-1980s a long-established working farm with a public house attached. The idea of a farm-cum-ale house was a very common feature well into the 20th century, and many of our rural inns started life this way. To increase their income it was quite usual for a farmer's wife to set herself up

The Mundy Arms, for many years a farm-cum-ale house and the only pub in the village. *(Author)*

The Mackworth Hotel, formerly, for a while, the home of architect Henry Isaac Stevens and later the Clark-Maxwell family when they inherited the estate. *(Author)*

as the local brewer to make a little extra money on the side. As the nearest pub to the Mundy Arms in those days was the Nimrod and Hotspur in Markeaton village, a place nearer home was welcome. This latter establishment, which closed *c.*1904, is still there, having been converted to an attractive cottage, but the brewhouse which stood close by was demolished in 1997 as it was declared to be unsafe. The signboard also existed until the second half of the 20th century when it was regrettably destroyed. The inn was named after a couple of racehorses. This house, like those adjoining it, contains reused timbers, which almost certainly came from the old hall when it was demolished.

Villages are, of course, nothing without people, whether native or incomers, and while Markeaton and Mackworth have no one of great national importance to talk about there are several of more local fame who should be a source of pride and interest for the community. Although emphasis has been put on the narrow way of life of the peasants, not all who were born here remained tied to the manor and among those who raised themselves above the average level of the working class was Richard Crowshawe (1561–1631) who was born at Mackworth, the son of the blacksmith of Markeaton. The position of village blacksmith was a very important one and Richard would have been assured of a relatively good living, but he wanted more and went to London to learn the art of silver and goldsmithing, thus emulating Sir John Mundy, his manorial lord's father. He was successful to the extent that he became very rich and achieved the ultimate accolade of his profession by being appointed sometime Master of the Worshipful Company of London Goldsmiths. In spite of his success he never forgot his origins and is credited with doing much good work tending the sick during the great plague of 1625 and in his will he also remembered the poor by leaving almost £5,000 to charities, an enormous sum in those days. One of the bequests appears below:

> ... by his will bearing date April 26 1631, directed the Bailiffs and Burgesses of the Borough of Derby, in consideration of a Legacy Hereby bequeathed to them to pay Twenty Eight pounds yearly for ever for a weekly distribution to eight poor ancient Inhabitants of the Towns of Mackworth and Markeaton in Bread, Cheese and Money, such poor to be nominated by the Parson Churchwardens and chief inhabitants of those places, and such remainder as should be left of his said Gift to

be given to the Clerk and Sexton. The said Richard Croshaw, by his said Will likewise gave to the said Bailiffs and Burgesses One Hundred Pounds, to be disposed of as loans to poor Householders and Tradesmen of the said Townships of Markeaton and Mackworth, who should be of good fame and reputation; the interest thereof is given yearly amongst the poorest Inhabitants of the said places, at the discretion of the Chief Parishoners. *(This extract is taken from the Benefactions Board in the north aisle of the church.)*

There is a monument to Richard Crowshawe on the north wall in Derby Cathedral which reads:

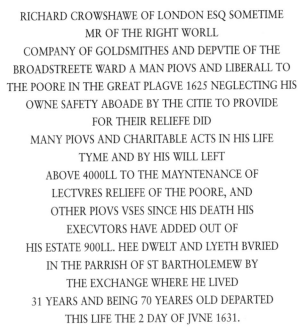

TO THE GLORY OF GOD

RICHARD CROWSHAWE OF LONDON ESQ SOMETIME
MR OF THE RIGHT WORLL
COMPANY OF GOLDSMITHES AND DEPVTIE OF THE
BROADSTREETE WARD A MAN PIOVS AND LIBERALL TO
THE POORE IN THE GREAT PLAGVE 1625 NEGLECTING HIS
OWNE SAFETY ABOADE BY THE CITIE TO PROVIDE
FOR THEIR RELIEFE DID
MANY PIOVS AND CHARITABLE ACTS IN HIS LIFE
TYME AND BY HIS WILL LEFT
ABOVE 4000LL TO THE MAYNTENANCE OF
LECTVRES RELIEFE OF THE POORE, AND
OTHER PIOVS VSES SINCE HIS DEATH HIS
EXECVTORS HAVE ADDED OUT OF
HIS ESTATE 900LL. HEE DWELT AND LYETH BVRIED
IN THE PARRISH OF ST BARTHOLEMEW BY
THE EXCHANGE WHERE HE LIVED
31 YEARS AND BEING 70 YEARES OLD DEPARTED
THIS LIFE THE 2 DAY OF JVNE 1631.

HAVING DONE MVCH GOOD TO THIS TOWNE
AND THIS HIS NATIVE COVNTRYE HIS EXECVTORS
HAVE ERECTED THIS MONVMENT IN THIS
PLACE TO ENCOVRAGE OTHERS OF GREAT
ESTATES TO IMNITAT HIS PYETYE
AND CHARITIE.
1636.

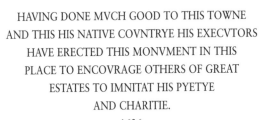

Two portraits of Samuel Richardson, one in formal attire and one in more relaxed mood without his wig. *(Derby Local Studies Library)*

Richard Crowshawe may have been the first locally recorded person to make such a bequest, but he was followed over many years by others and this sort of charity was still in operation well into the 20th century, as a friend of the author remembers being sent to the Mundy Arms to collect the allotted ration of bread.

Another man of local birth who achieved modest fame was Samuel Richardson, son of Samuel and Elizabeth, who was baptised at Mackworth on 19 August 1689. Samuel senior was a carpenter and joiner who had moved here from London to where, 10 years after Samuel junior's birth, the family returned. For a while young Samuel was educated at Christ's Hospital, but at the age of 17 he was apprenticed to a printer and by his early thirties he had progressed well enough to set himself up in the trade in Fleet Street, from where he became one of London's leading printers, even doing work for the House of Commons. In 1740, at the age of 50, he became a novelist, something quite rare in those days when the vast majority of the population were illiterate and elitism among the upper classes permitted little apart from religious or classical reading. As an example, in her will of 16 July 1611, Jane Mundy left to her son '… Mr Smith's sermons to exercise him and his children thereupon'. Who Mr Smith was is not clear, as there was at no time an incumbent of that name at Mackworth. Richardson's first novel was entitled *Pamela or Virtue Rewarded* and was a moral and, for those days, explicit story of a young servant girl who resisted the overtly physical advances of the son of the house and was eventually rewarded with her virtue intact and a wedding ring on her finger. Little did he realise while writing that he had created an international bestseller, and he became one of the first recipients of fan mail. His next book, *Clarissa*, filled seven volumes and was produced in instalments during 1747–48, stretching to over a million words, still a record for an English novel. Considered to be his masterpiece, it unfortunately did not have a happy ending, the heroine finally committing suicide in spite of pleas from the reading public to let her live. His final work, *Sir Charles Grandison*, was written in 1753–54 and was destined to become a favourite of Jane Austen. Richardson died on 4 July 1761, leaving an estate of £14,000, not bad for the son of a carpenter from a small agricultural village near Derby.

Some members of the Mundy family possessed artistic talents and Francis Noel Clark (1739–1815) was no exception. He wrote poetry, including, in 1776, a long poem entitled *Needwood Forest* and followed it a few years later with *The Fall of Needwood*. They were published for private circulation in the early 19th century, beautifully bound and illustrated by Drewry of Derby. The author has seen a copy with the inscribed book plate of Harriot Georgiana Mundy, the wife of Francis Noel Clark's grandson, so this was her personal possession. This edition has some additional short poems, one to his grandson William 'on his repeating to me most perfectly and accurately my poem *The Fall of Needwood*, which he had secretly got by heart' and another which extols the virtues of R.R. Reinagle, the artist of the picture on page 31.

Lancelot 'Capability' Brown is well known as the leading English 18th-century designer

Bowbridge House, the 'good brick house' built by William Emes *c.*1765. Having arrived by stagecoach one wonders what his thoughts would be regarding the vehicle now parked on his drive. *(Author)*

of landscapes and some writers give the impression that he was the only one at that time. However, he actually had several very talented though less celebrated contemporaries and of these William Emes (1729–1803) was among the foremost. His early life is obscure as he was born of now unknown parents at an equally unknown locale, although the Church Broughton area of Derbyshire is sometimes tentatively suggested. How he became a gardener and architect and where he trained are yet more mysteries, but the thought of him being apprenticed at Markeaton in the days of Wrightson Mundy is a very tempting and pleasant one; he certainly seems to have found favour there. His letter-writing shows that he was well educated and that may also be the result of his association with Wrightson, who would not have been slow to recognise and encourage talent. By 1756 Emes was working at Kedleston, as the Curzon family accounts record his arrival there from London with his manservant. In 1759 he married Mary Innocent and the following year he set up independently and also acquired a lease on some land at Bowbridge, where he subsequently built, or rebuilt, in around 1765, a 'good brick house', Bowbridge House, which still stands and certainly merits his description. Emes spread his talents locally at Foremark, Markeaton, Calke Abbey, Darley Abbey and St Helen's House in Derby, while continuing to freelance at Kedleston. Later he worked further afield in Staffordshire and Wales. In 1790 he moved to Elvetham Park in Hampshire, while retaining his lease of Bowbridge, and worked until 1795, the date of his last known commission. He died in London in March 1803.

A Derby magistrate, Gervase Bennet owned land in the manor in the 17th century; he it was who, at the trial of George Fox, founded the Society of Friends and dubbed them 'Quakers', a title they have borne ever since.

George Selwyn Clark-Maxwell (1900–1990), known locally simply as CM, inherited the estate in 1935 on the death of his father, the Revd William Gilchrist Clark-Maxwell. His career included astronomy and optical engineering before he became a doctor and specialised in brain surgery, of which he was a brilliant exponent. He founded the Neurological Unit at the Derbyshire Royal Infirmary (since transferred to the Queen's Medical Centre in Nottingham) and was a founder member and one-time president of the British Neurological Society. He is mentioned again in the section *Afterthought* at the end of this book.

On the subject of local people, Mrs Emily Mundy relates this remarkable political incident:

Mr William Mundy stood for Parliament after the death of Edward Mundy of Shipley, who died at Barbados in January 1849, and on March 23rd he was duly elected and no one opposed him. In the election of 1859 the Hon. Augustus Vernon stood against Mr Mundy, who was advised by his Committee to vote for himself; no one suggested it to Mr Vernon, and Mr Mundy was elected by one vote. I believe that coming in by one's own vote is looked on as quite unique.

Henry Tunnicliffe and his wife Mary Ann, daughter Mary and son Harry with the family pets. Henry worked on the estate as a woodman and he also appears at the right-hand side of the photograph in the wood yard on page 78. *(Private collection)*

Figures at the county elections of 1859:

*T.W. Evans	3,536
*W. Mundy	3,185
Hon. Augustus Vernon	3,184

*Elected

Watercolour showing the view from the hall in 1926, painted by Emily Mundy when she was 80. Some trees had been removed on Markeaton Lane as Mackworth Church is visible left of centre. On the back she wrote; 'To Tunnicliffe to show the view he has created'. Mrs Mundy often gave gifts of this nature. *(Private collection)*

Some families have long connections with the manor and can be traced through parish records for several hundred years. Among these are the names Ambrose, Bennett, Bryer, Colbourn (to which the author has a distant connection), Gilman, Hanson, Haslam,

A family group in Mackworth in the 1880s. William Bull with his wife Eleanor and their children pose outside their cottage next to the 'castle'. *(Private collection)*

Hinchcliffe (two of whom were priests of the parish) Pickering, (three of whom were priests of the parish) and Spalton. The first named family originated in Pinfold Lane, later moved to Derby, and actually acquired property to the extent of owning a row of houses near Friargate, which are still known as Ambrose Terrace. A detailed study tracing the Ambrose family from the 17th century was made by Rosemary Lucas and published in 1998 as a monograph, *Pinfold Lane Cottages, Mackworth*. At one time there were six families named Smith in the parish who had no known connection with each other.

A couple of light-hearted entries, both responsibly vouched for, seem worth including in this section on people. The first concerns the Revd William Gilchrist Clark-Maxwell, who, in common with many people, suffered some loss of hearing in later life. At the crucial point of a christening he asked 'Name this child'. Rather quietly the mother replied 'Lucy, sir'. 'Lucifer?' responded the Reverend, 'certainly not, I shall name him John!'

Secondly, Mackworth was for a while home to a man who was not famous but who thought he should have been. The Revd Harry Dane, who was Priest in Charge here from 1979 till 1987, considered that he should have been in the *Guinness Book of Records* as he claimed to be the only man ever to have been forced off his bicycle by a flying aeroplane. And live! 'I leapt from my bike and fell face down. The plane came down, crushed my bike and missed me by inches'. This incident occurred at Bexhill in his younger days.

It would not be possible to properly conclude this section without giving some space to Mrs Emily Mundy, the last resident of Markeaton Hall, whose name has already appeared

The Bull family again, this time in the yard behind the 'castle' gateway, possibly on the occasion of the marriage of their daughter Anne to William Mansfield on 16 October 1893. *(Private collection)*

Three local lads in the church field *c.*1890. It is interesting to note that the one on the right is wearing glasses. *(Private collection)*

briefly on several occasions in previous pages. While researching for this book the author was privileged to meet a number of people who had worked for her or who had lived on the estate during her time as lady of the manor and who had vivid memories of her. What emerged was a picture of a very mixed personality, a woman who was autocratic, the absolute mistress of all she owned, who made the rules and who demanded unquestioning obedience and loyalty from her employees. One of those rules was that domestic staff in the hall dressed for dinner. In return she proved to be kindly, considerate and generous to her people, at least by the standards of the early 20th century. As an example of her autocracy, she would walk to Mackworth church, accompanied by all available members of her staff, along the gravel path already mentioned under *Roads* which, as also mentioned, had been thoroughly raked the previous day. On reaching the church her bailiff would enter by the south door in the chancel and his arrival brought the assembled congregation to their feet. Mrs Mundy then entered and took her place in the chancel stalls, where she would say her private prayers, after which a nod from the bailiff was sufficient for the service to begin. At the end the congregation again stood while Mrs Mundy departed and another nod from the bailiff allowed them to relax and say their own final private prayers.

Another instance of her power was related by the late Miss Arnett, who lived for over 70 years at the School House on Markeaton Lane. In her very young days she and her sister were playing on the lane when they saw, in the distance, Mrs Mundy's coach approaching. Rather than stand and curtsey as was expected of them they dived into the nearest ditch and stayed there till the coach had passed, a move they were later to regret. On arriving home they were soundly spanked by their father on the orders of Mrs Mundy, who proved to have very sharp eyes!

When she went shopping in Derby she would direct her coachman to the appropriate shop and remain in the coach while the shopkeeper was made aware of her presence. He would then be apprised of her requirements and his staff quickly brought out samples for her inspection. From these she would select whatever was required and order its delivery before telling the coachman to proceed to the next destination, all without actually looking at, or speaking directly to, the shop staff.

Although motor cars were becoming fashionable she never had one, remaining faithful to her landau and two horses throughout her life. She must have regretted this one day early in World War One when, on a visit to Derby, the army commandeered her horses!

A special edition Royal Crown Derby plate commissioned by Emily Mundy as seasonal gifts for the estate workers, Christmas 1924. Only 50 were made. *(Author)*

Her kindlier side showed as she ensured that no one on her estate ever went short of necessities such as bread and coal, even if they could not work. That may not seem very much by today's standards, but then it meant a great deal. The marriage of a tenant was treated as a festive occasion, with all attending the wedding dressed in their best. At Christmas there were gifts of poultry and the like and one year she commissioned a limited edition Royal Crown Derby plate for each tenant, some of which still exist as valuable collectors' pieces. In her later years the park was opened to the public on one day a year, quite a treat for many working-class people who normally saw little apart from crowded streets, tiny back yards and factories and, as we have seen in the section on Markeaton Hall, she eventually left it to them and us.

Remembered with respect and affection by those who knew her, Mrs Mundy was also known to be something of an eccentric. On one occasion while driving through Mackworth she stopped the coach by Mackworth House Farm and commented that the upstairs needed a central window adding as it didn't look right as it was. This proved to be structurally impossible, but her word was law and something had to be done. In practice a false window was mounted on the outside of the house and remained there until after her death. There was apparently no danger of her ever condescending to go inside to check. The light mark it left can still be seen between the upper windows. (See page 117)

In her writings in *Varieties* Mrs Mundy touches on many subjects, from her ancestors to travel, the social round, politics, servants' wages and the state of the poorer classes, for whom she seems to have had a genuine concern. Today the media give much time and space to sports, especially football and the excessive salaries given to players and the resultant high prices paid by fans to watch them. This is not new. In 1909 Mrs Mundy wrote:

Then again, luxury has increased in all classes – in dress, in food, in amusements. What an amount of money, for instance, is always found for football! At the moment children may be starving, but the money must be found for the man to go to a football match. This sounds severe, but I know that it was true in a big town last winter; prices which would not be paid for anything else were readily paid for admission to the football ground, and of the crowds who were there, many had no money for food at their homes.

Mrs Mundy also commented frequently on the weather, proving that then, as today, it was very much a British social talking point and that the situation has changed very little since. Of 1846, (presumably quoting her predecessor, Harriot Mundy) she wrote:

The winter was very extra-ordinary. Up to the middle of March there was no cold, the cuckoo was heard in Derbyshire and a swarm of bees seen in Hampshire; then from the middle of March, snow and rain, and the ice-house filled on the 21st of March, and the white thorns round the ice-house were in leaf and showing flowers. Nobody remembers such a winter.

In 1849 there was another bad spring, 'During April very cold, much snow in Dorsetshire and London, and bitterly cold up to the 21st June.'

Emily Mundy's concern for the poor continued. Not far from the eastern boundary of the park was that part of Derby known as the West End (built on what was formerly part of the park), of which much has been said and written, frequently with an air of nostalgia for what has gone but without any noticeable desire to go back. It was a large area crammed full of small, low-grade housing, of which poverty, overcrowding and hardship were integral features, though these in turn bred a close-knit community spirit it would be difficult to emulate elsewhere. A more stark contrast between these conditions and the spacious luxury over the fence to the west would be hard to imagine and, purely for survival, poaching on the estate and further afield was a regular occupation for some West Enders. Mrs Mundy must have been sensitive to this contrast to the extent that, in 1909, in memory of her late husband, she donated four and a half acres of land for the use of the people of the West End. This became the Mackworth Recreation Grounds and adjoined the allotment gardens given by Francis Noel Mundy some years previously. Allotment gardens were essential for many people for growing vegetables cheaply and there were hundreds of them available on the estate for an annual rental of three shillings. There was a large area of them on the triangular field by the Play Centre and across Ashbourne Road, to the south, several fields were given over to allotments. The author's grandfather and father had adjacent ones on Windmill Hill Lane, but the site is now lost under the school playground on Walthamstow Road on Mackworth Estate. Mrs Mundy's new recreation facilities, which were restricted in use to children under the age of 10 and elderly people, included sports fields, a

Children playing in the Markeaton Brook in the Mackworth Recreation Ground c.1908. Thirty yards to the right of this picture, on the other side of the road, a swimming pool was made by widening and damming the brook.

The sad remains of the swimming pool provided by Emily Mundy for the people of the West End of Derby. There were changing cubicles for males on one side and for females on the other. *(Author)*

playground and a dam across the brook to form a swimming pool, albeit for summer use only! Quite what use the elderly made of those facilities is left to the imagination. The brook was to remain unfenced for children to sail their toy boats. With the exception of the swimming pool these facilities are still in use, though now more for the public in general, the West End having been cleared and replaced by modern housing.

The final word must be, for many people, a discordant one. In 1983 the extension to the A38 trunk road was built across the north-east corner of the park. This raised cries of 'Vandalism', 'Desecration' and so on, and certainly a lot of property and trees were destroyed. There is no intention here to get involved in argument about the rights and wrongs of the situation. In spite of the realities, many of the objections to it were probably biased by nostalgia, a desire to live our lives through in familiar, stable surroundings and to leave things 'as they were'. But for how long have things been 'as they were'? In the timescale of the last 2,000 years the answer to the question has to be 'not very long', and already there is a generation of young adults who have no memory of what many of us feel we have lost. The road is there whether we like it or not, and if we care to look back it can be seen as just one more piece in the ever-changing kaleidoscopic pattern of the landscape. Maybe, when the Romans arrived in the district 19 and a half centuries ago, the local natives expressed similar sentiments when they found that an unwanted road was being built through their land!

Afterthought

The foregoing is, hopefully, the basic outline history of the manors of Markeaton and Mackworth. The first edition of 1987 was well complemented in 1995 by Rosemary Lucas's book *The Manor of Markeaton, Mackworth & Allestree*, covering in detail the period 1650–1851, which, as her research proves, is reasonably well documented. However, the Roman period and the early Dark Age days when the villages were first founded remain barren of hard historical fact, a situation which can be only partially relieved by comparing with other places in the country for which some documentary and physical evidence has survived. This void in our knowledge leads inevitably to feelings of disappointment and frustration. Having read the first book, Dr Clark-Maxwell assured me that I should not be concerned by this as he knew the true origins of these two villages. He was a man of deep religious conviction, with a love of his village and countryside coupled with a distinct sense of humour, all three of which clearly shine through in his version:

> In the beginning God created the heaven and the earth; and the earth was without form, and void; and darkness was upon the face of the deep. And God said 'Let there be light' and there was light. And a similar thing happened at Markeaton and Mackworth...

While I still suspect that my mundane version is nearer the truth I have to confess to a preference for the second one!

Don Farnsworth
March 2006

Bibliography

A History of the English Parish N.J.G.Pounds, Cambridge University Press, 2000.

Allestree, from Adelard to Raphael, J.W.Allen.

Along Long Lane Don Farnsworth, 2003.

A Stage or Two Beyond Christendom, Revd Michael Austin, 2001.

A Summary of the Enclosure Act and Award for the Manor of Markeaton, Mackworth and Allestree, 1760–1763, Rosemary Lucas, unpublished.

Britannia, Vol. XIV, 1983, Shimon Appelbaum re 'discrete manors'.

Burdett, *Map of Derbyshire*, 1767 and 1791.

Churches of Derbyshire, four volumes, Dr J. Charles Cox, 1877.

Citizens' Derby, Dr Alfred Richardson, 1948.

Darley Cartulary, Editor Professor R. Darlington.

Derbyshire Archaelogical Journal, Vols. 51, 1930 and 101, 1981.

Derbyshire Charters, I.H. Jeayes, 1906.

Derbyshire Directories, Various.

Deserted Villages, Rowley and Wood, Shire Publications.

Domesday, A Search for the Roots of England, Michael Wood, 1986.

Domesday Book. Various editions.

English Society in the Early Middle Ages, Doris Mary Stenton, 1985, Pelican Books.

Fields in the English Landscape, C. Taylor.

Hanged for Three Pennies, E. Garner, 2000.

Magna Britannia, Vol. 5, Derbyshire, Revd Daniel and Samuel Lysons, 1817.

Medieval Fields, Hall, Shire Publications.

Mundy-Lysons Scrapbooks, Harriot Mundy, 1868.

Peakland Roads and Trackways, A.E. and E.M. Dodd, 1974.

Pinfold Lane Cottages, Mackworth, Rosemary Lucas, 1998.

Place Names of Derbyshire, K. Cameron, 1957.

Roman Roads of Britain, Ivan Margary, 1967.

The Beginnings of English Society, Dorothy Whitelock, 1954, Pelican Books.

The Derby School Register, 1570-1901. Editor B. Taccella.

The Derbyshire Country House, Craven and Stanley, 1991.

The Friargate Line, Mark Higginson, 1989.

The History and Antiquities of the County of Surrey, Vol. 1, Revd Owen Manning and William Bray, 1804.

The History of Derbyshire, four volumes, Gladwyn Turbutt, 1999.

The Manor of Markeaton, Mackworth and Allestree, 1650–1851, Rosemary Lucas, 1995.

Village and Farmstead, C. Taylor.

Further complementary reading:

West End Story, Elsie Elizabeth Goodhead.

Tales of a Derby Poacher, Tom Gwinutt.

Larkrise to Candleford, Flora Thompson. This is a very readable first-hand account of country life in Oxfordshire during the 19th century and, while it is admittedly not local, the prevailing situations there and in this area must have been very similar.